In Trump We Trust

In Trump We Trust

E Pluribus Awesome!

Ann Coulter

SENTINEL

An imprint of Penguin Random House LLC
375 Hudson Street
New York, New York 10014

Copyright © 2016 Ann Coulter
Penguin supports copyright. Copyright fuels creativity, encourages
diverse voices, promotes free speech, and creates a vibrant culture.
Thank you for buying an authorized edition of this book and for complying
with copyright laws by not reproducing, scanning, or distributing
any part of it in any form without permission. You are supporting writers
and allowing Penguin to continue to publish books for every reader.

LIBRARY OF CONGRESS CATALOGING-IN-PUBLICATION DATA
Names: Coulter, Ann H., author.
Title: In Trump We Trust / Ann Coulter.
Description: New York, New York: Sentinel, 2016. |
Includes bibliographical references and index.
Identifiers: LCCN 2016030187 | ISBN 9780735214460 (hardback)
Subjects: LCSH: Trump, Donald, 1946– | Trump, Donald, 1946–Political and
social views. | Presidential candidates–United States–Biography. |
Presidents–United States–Election–2016. | Republican Party (U.S. 1854–) |
United States–Politics and government–2009- | BISAC: POLITICAL
SCIENCE / Political Ideologies / Conservatism & Liberalism. | POLITICAL
SCIENCE / Political Process / Political Parties.
Classification: LCC E901.1.T78 C68 2016 | DDC 973.932092 [B] –dc23
LC record available at https://lccn.loc.gov/2016030187

Printed in the United States of America
1   3   5   7   9   10   8   6   4   2

To: Mickey Kaus

ACKNOWLEDGMENTS

I didn't have time to force as many friends as I'd like to read any portion this book, but I did trick some into reading a few chapters and I thank them deeply: Ned Rice, Rodney Conover, Trish Baker, Kevin Harrington, Mickey Kaus, Jon Tukel, and Jim Moody. And thank you to my agent Mel Berger and my publisher Adrian Zackheim for agreeing to this lightning speed project, and everyone at Penguin Random House who worked so hard to produce a book—and audio!—in record time: Eric Nelson, Jessica Kaye, Will Weisser, Tara Gilbride, Vivian Roberson, Victoria Miller, and Tess Espinoza.

Contents

CHAPTER ONE
Trump: The Great Orange Hope   1

CHAPTER TWO
The Reality TV Star We've Been Waiting For!   12

CHAPTER THREE
First Principle of the GOP: "Who Asked You?"   22

CHAPTER FOUR
Political Consultants' Three-Card Monte   38

CHAPTER FIVE
I Don't Care What They Say, I Won't Stay in a World
Without Trump   54

CHAPTER SIX
You're Not Reagan   65

CHAPTER SEVEN
No Policy Specifics!   79

CHAPTER EIGHT
Trump Hits Back   96

CHAPTER NINE
Disabled Reporter Joins Media Effort to Create More
Disabled Americans   112

CHAPTER TEN
Islam's PR Agency: The American Media   125

CHAPTER ELEVEN
Now We Know Why They Don't
Want to Talk about Muslim Immigration   137

CHAPTER TWELVE
So Close!
The Plan to Destroy America Was Almost Complete   154

CHAPTER THIRTEEN
Trump Builds Wall, Makes GOP Pay for It   167

CHAPTER FOURTEEN
The New Trumpian Party!   180

Appendix: Geniuses   183

Notes   199

CHAPTER ONE

Trump:
The Great Orange Hope

Until June 16, 2015, every conservative felt four things:

1. We're losing.
2. The fight wasn't fair—it was over before it began, and the rules were rigged.
3. Our allies have abandoned us.
4. This loss is permanent. We're not getting it back.

Plug in any issue and it works: abortion, gay marriage, transgender bathrooms, immigration, trade, Press 1 for English, drug legalization, criminal law, the Iraq War, and on and on.

By 2012, Obama's 2008 position on gay marriage, as "the union between a man and a woman,"[1] had become the vicious Klan position, a transformation unparalleled in the physical universe.

Fifty years ago, American traitor Bradley Manning would have been executed within a week. Instead, taxpayers are footing the bill for his sexual reassignment surgery.

In the 2008 presidential race, every single Democrat but one opposed driver's licenses for illegal aliens[2]—Hillary, Barack Obama, John Edwards, and Joe Biden. By 2012 illegal aliens could get a driver's license in forty-nine states, as a result of Obama's "executive amnesty." The only holdout was Nebraska—and the ACLU was suing Nebraska.

The mayor of Los Angeles brags that more than two hundred languages are spoken in his city.[3] A majority of the residents speak a language other than English at home.[4] Fifty years ago, even Democrats would have said that's insane. Today, Republicans are afraid to criticize it.[5]

In 2012, the most attractive candidate Republicans had run for president in three decades lost in a blowout defeat to President Obama, a feckless incumbent who wrecked health care and whose foreign policies had resulted in Islamic lunatics murdering the American ambassador in Benghazi less than two months before the election. There was no way to minimize what a disaster Mitt Romney's loss was. Looking ahead to possible 2016 presidential candidates, it was gun-to-the-mouth time.

It's just been wave after wave hitting the bow. Americans were huddled on the battleship *Missouri,* having surrendered everything they believe in, hoping it would all go away.

Is it really any wonder that when a space capsule crashed to earth and Donald J. Trump stepped out, he was given a warm welcome?

Trump is the first hope Americans have had in a very long time that it may not be over yet. Perhaps the country isn't finished. Maybe we could begin to reverse our losses. And then, many years from now, when we have our country back, we will join the little girls in pink party dresses and be appalled by a presidential candidate who calls Rosie O'Donnell a "fat pig" and sends out juvenile tweets at midnight.

But not yet, not until Trump ends the orderly transition of

America from the greatest nation in history into some pathetic, third-rate, also-ran, multicultural mess. Until the bleeding has stopped, there's nothing Trump can do that won't be forgiven. Except change his immigration policies.

Even liberals know that Trump is the only impediment to their destruction of America. In May 2016, Harvard law professor Mark Tushnet let out a war whoop to his fellow liberals, proclaiming total victory. "The culture wars," he said, "are over; they lost, we won." With conservatives standing there, asking the burglar if we could keep our underwear, Tushnet said the left should be merciless, citing LGBT activists as exemplars of the "hard-line approach." He reminded liberals that Justice Anthony Kennedy was irrelevant now that Justice Antonin Scalia was dead, saying: *"fuck Anthony Kennedy."* Finally, he proposed that liberals draw up a list of Supreme Court decisions targeted for reversal. (Topping Hillary's list is *District of Columbia v. Heller,* which would effectively repeal the Second Amendment.)

But at the end of the piece, Tushnet concluded: "Of course all bets are off if Donald Trump becomes President."[6]

IF YOU BUILD IT, THEY WON'T COME

Trump announced he was running for president in a speech talking about Mexican rapists, pledging to deport illegal aliens and build a wall. He said America was getting ripped off in its trade deals with China, Japan, and Mexico, and that he was running because the country would soon be so far gone, it would be unsalvageable.

The media reacted as if he'd called for gas chambers, but that speech propelled Trump to the top of the polls. So the pundits furrowed their brows and explained that Trump was "riding a wave of anger against Washington," there was "anger sweeping America," his supporters "are fed up with the status quo," he was appealing to "this very visceral, very angry populist working class blue collar worker." (Actual quotes—I'm too busy to footnote.) Evidently, voters were angry. Lots of anger. Fiery pits of anger. The 2016 electorate would have made Sam Kinison president.

On the other hand, if it was just tough talk the voters were hungering for, why didn't Governor Chris Christie go anywhere? He wasn't exactly Cary Grant on the campaign trail.

One must consider the possibility that it was Trump's policies the voters liked. His announcement speech about Mexican rapists and building a wall may have appalled the media and the political class, but the voters were ecstatic.

Month after month, at every rally, whenever Trump mentioned the wall, the crowds went wild. It was Trump's one sure-fire standing ovation, his "Free Bird" at a Lynyrd Skynyrd concert. Even before Trump would take the stage, his supporters would start chanting "BUILD THE WALL!" He'd do callbacks with the audience on the wall, asking, "And who's going to pay for it?" Crowd: "MEXICO!" *Daily Beast* columnist Michael Moynihan tweeted: "Talked to lots of Trump supporters in Iowa. When I pointed out he wasn't a conservative, all had same answer: 'So? The wall!'"[7]

Trump speaks in exciting, declarative sentences, giving voters any number of possible chants. Based on the policies so deeply hidden in his speeches and policy papers that our media couldn't find them, Trump's crowds could have started chanting:

Bomb ISIS!
Take their oil!
Bring our jobs home!
Make China pay!

Repeal Obamacare!
Protect the Second Amendment!
Repeal Common Core!
Let's get tired of winning!
Concealed carry!
Protect our veterans!
Make our country rich!
Bring back the American dream!
Make America great again!

But that's not what they chanted. They certainly weren't chanting "Reform Social Security!" or "Protect Ukraine's national sovereignty!" No, the slogan that inspired a million T-shirts, chalk etchings, replicas, and hashtags was: *Build the wall!*

I'm beginning to suspect the wall is popular.

Although the media tried to portray Trump's popularity as a cult of personality, ironically, the one thing voters weren't wild about was his personality. Trump was a huge reality TV star long before he announced for president. He'd been threatening a presidential run for at least a decade. And yet, before kicking off his campaign, he was in single digits in Iowa.[8] Then he gave that speech.

The media were dying to call Trump's immigration policies "racist," and he tricked them into trying—with the GOP helping. Unfortunately for the media and the Republican Brain Trust, Trump's policies were popular with all kinds of voters. It wasn't just "angry white men" who were losing jobs to wage-depressing, admittedly hardworking, Mexicans. So were black people. So were Hispanics—at least a third of who oppose amnesty.

It's one thing to push an unpopular idea. The GOP does that all the time: the Trans-Pacific Partnership, privatizing Social Security—how about the Iraq War? Trump's genius was that he was pushing policies that were popular. The fact that the media said they weren't just made him look brave. He used the media's lies against them.

Political analysts kept droning on and on about Trump's mysterious appeal, but in all their prolix analyses, I can't find a single one saying, BOY, WERE WE WRONG ABOUT IMMIGRATION!

None of the media's usual attacks on Republicans worked with Trump. He wasn't a Holy Roller, pastor-in-chief type. Far from protecting the rich, he wanted to raise taxes on Wall Street and save Social Security. Nothing about him was conceivably threatening to swing voters. He never tried to show off to some tiny group by saying stupid things like, *Of course I'm okay with banning abortion in cases of rape and incest!* He opposed abortion, but supported Planned Parenthood's other work. He had a slew of black celebrity endorsements and the stalwart admiration of YouTube phenomenon Diamond and Silk. He opposed the Iraq War, a massively popular position now that Obama has turned our victory there into a defeat and the birthplace of ISIS.

Liberals had to throw away their usual playbook against the GOP with Trump. For decades, it's been the same thing every four years: Republicans are the "party of the rich," itching to start wars abroad and impose a theocracy at home. Trump lives on Fifth Avenue and is married to a model. Are you really worried there's going to be compulsory Bible reading? Conservative pundits could only rail that Trump wasn't a "real Republican." After the past few decades, most voters said, *Fantastic! Thanks for reminding me.*

Trump's defining issue was the one elites in both parties steadfastly refused to address: the public's desire for less immigration. All they could do was sputter—*this is too silly, he's a reality TV star, you can't be serious.* If you were the paranoid type, you might suspect that the media were trying to avoid the topic. It was easier to tell themselves fairy tales about Trump's rise being a result of his celebrity, or because of some nonspecific anger toward "the establishment," than to admit it was all about—or even a teeny tiny bit about—immigration.

There are other issues, but they all come down to the same thing: taking America's side—on trade, on war, on outsourcing, on NAFTA, on NATO, on our borders, on terrorism. It just happens that none have been so furiously resisted by both Republicans and Democrats as taking America's side on immigration.

Trump's victory was not a fluke, not a "summer fling," not a name recognition contest. Voters were fed up with illegal immigration, fed up with refugees, fed up with legal immigrants who show their gratitude by gunning down Americans. They wanted a champion who wouldn't betray them. No matter how much the media and the political class yelled at Trump and demanded apologies, he never backed down.

None of the other candidates could approach Trump on immigration because they were dependent on wealthy contributors. Their advisers begged them, *Please, PLEASE, do not touch immigration!* Some Republicans surely knew in their hearts that dumping millions of low-wage workers on America was hurting the people who lived here, but they were too scared of not getting the fat checks to say so.

Trump was in the weird position of not needing big donors. He's beholden to no one except the millions of ordinary Americans showing up at his speeches, following him on Twitter, and giving him more primary votes than any Republican in history.

He will have no obligation to anyone, except the people. They're the ones who will have put him in the White House. The pundits, think tanks, and "conservative" media made sure of that. The reason regular Americans get turned off by politics is that no one ever pays attention to them. This time, there will be a bond between the president and the people. House Speaker Paul Ryan thinks he can bollix up Trump on the wall or trade deals? Wait until Trump hops on Twitter.

If Trump is elected president, he will be the richest man ever to hold that office and, in modern times, the one who spent the least amount of money to get there. In addition to putting a crimp in *The New York Times'* never-ending series on the danger of "money in politics," this might finally force Republicans to notice that the one thing they need even more than money is voters.

AMERICANS ARE HOMESICK

Liberals compulsively demand the constant importation of foreigners because of their seething hatred of the historic American nation. They won't be happy until the DAR-eligible population is a tiny minority. Any culture that replaces American culture is an improvement, as far as they are concerned.

Why shouldn't Americans fight to preserve their culture? All of us have a place that we think of as home. People from the most economically depressed, physically dilapidated, stultifyingly boring, intellectually backward places will always say of their hometowns, "It was a good place to grow up." Los Angeles's public TV station KCET runs a beloved program called *Things That Aren't Here Anymore,* featuring great Hollywood restaurants of yesteryear, a park for pony rides that used to be in the middle of Beverly Hills, and so on. All of us, no matter what our circumstances, feel powerfully connected to our home.

Other people are allowed to have a home. Americans traveling abroad are encouraged to leave as small a footprint as possible, especially where there's a so-called indigenous population. We're terrified of trampling on the dominant culture or being seen as Clem from Texas. To the average liberal, "ugly American" is redundant.

Why are Americans embarrassed to ask for ketchup at a French café if there's no such thing as a national culture with distinctive characteristics? If a person says he loves Paris, do we assume it's just the architecture? Or is it how Parisians dress, cook, speak, and live their lives? When you want to take a vacation, does the travel agent ask you where you want to go, or just offer to book the cheapest flight anywhere, as if there's no difference between Holland and Colombia?

Americans are the only ones who aren't allowed to be nostalgic for things that define our home.

Politicians are constantly praising everyone's culture—except our own. Most Hispanics, Rand Paul effuses, "go to church and believe in traditional values."[9] Jeb Bush cut a campaign ad where he said, in Spanish: "To me, Hispanic culture is very important and positive."[10] Kasich said Hispanics "are God-fearing, hardworking folks." (He later added, "That's why in the hotel you leave a little tip.")[11] Hillary generalizes about Hispanics in her autobiography, saying, "Hispanics in South Texas were, understandably, wary of a blond girl from Chicago," and praises the Mexican delicacy, barbecued goat head.[12]

Clearly, it's perfectly acceptable to make generalizations about a people when being positive and pandering. Only generalizations that are negative—about anyone other than Americans—constitute hate crimes.

"Muslims are peaceful."—ACCEPTABLE.
"Muslims are violent."—HATE CRIME.
"Americans are violent."—ACCEPTABLE.
"Americans are peaceful."—NATIVIST.

Stripped of the argument that generalizations are out of bounds, we can get on with evaluating whether it's a good idea or a bad idea to jettison our own culture for another one. The left fully believes there is nothing worse than Americans, so anybody we replace an American with makes the country better. It's exactly the opposite of the truth.

Of all the places in the history of world, this is the culture that gleams and works the best. There's a reason the Magna Carta and the Glorious Revolution happened where they happened and that the Declaration of Independence was written in a British colony. It's not in the Anglo-Saxon character either to take orders or to give them. That's why the socialist left finally gave up on traditional Americans and pinned their hopes on immigrants, who bring their socialism with them.

As America diversifies, we might get better restaurants, but one of the negatives is that we pick up a lot more corruption. At its founding, America was populated by the most law-abiding people on the planet. It tells you something that, until the 1965 immigration act, the most problematic immigrants were the Irish. The same way virtually any immigrant to Finland makes it less white, almost any immigrant to America makes it less honest.

It's a cultural thing. British, Germans, and Scandinavians are the most honest. France is relatively corrupt—we always hear about the high taxes in France, but no one pays them. Italy and Greece are laughably corrupt. Except for Japan, no country in Asia is less corrupt than Italy. Every transaction between a citizen and a government official in Mexico involves a cash bribe. It's not just their governments that are corrupt—governments are only a reflection of the people. And we're bringing other people here by the millions.

Guess which Western European country has the highest rate of rape? Sweden. Rape used to be unheard of in Sweden. But it got boring looking at all those beautiful women and handsome men, so Sweden decided to import millions of third world people.

We talk about "democracy" in the rest of the world, but elsewhere "democracy" is defined as: seizing control of the government to benefit your friends. *Yes, we love democracy! I say whatever I need to say to get elected, in order to take government jobs away from people who aren't my relatives, and give them to people who are my relatives.* Immigrant criminal conspiracies are much more difficult to crack because of these famous "family values." Other ethnic groups can run vast, family-based international drug rings without fear of exposure. In America, David Greenglass's testimony sent his sister to the electric chair.

For both nostalgic and purely logical reasons, we should be powerfully defensive of what we have. We allow everyone else in the world to have a home, even though theirs are far less successful than ours. Only Americans are supposed to be embarrassed about their country and happy to see it destroyed.

Conservationists correctly point out that once a species is gone, it's gone. There's no getting it back. As Western Europe is discovering, the same is true of countries. If Trump loses, at least we'll finally know: it was too late. The left had too much time to bring in ringers and change the country's demographics. Between Teddy Kennedy's 1965 immigration act and the media making it a thought crime to want to preserve our culture, they've destroyed America.

Until June 16, 2015, there was no one to oppose them. If Trump is not elected president, it will be gone and Americans will be homesick forever.

I just want to have my answer. Is the country already finished?

CHAPTER TWO

The Reality TV Star We've Been Waiting For!

Everything that seems like a disability with Trump always turns out to be an advantage. If we were in the laboratory, designing the perfect presidential candidate, it's unlikely we would have produced a tasteless, publicity-seeking, coarse, billionaire, reality TV star.

Ha! Look at how wrong we were. It turns out, that is *exactly* what we needed.

The Miss Grundys of the party all say, *I'll tell you this, Donald Trump frightens me. He's a vulgarian, a loudmouth, a boor.* If the GOP's real complaint with Trump is that they think he can't win because of the trophy wives, the divorces, the bad grammar, and the gold fixtures, then why haven't they been able to produce another candidate without those problems but with Trump's issues?

They claim they don't mind Trump's positions on immigration and trade—they just wanted a candidate more like Mitt Romney to take them. That's a creature that doesn't exist in nature. Close your eyes and try to imagine Romney saying the things Trump has said. He couldn't survive two minutes of the abuse.

The problem with trying to find an old-school WASPy, understated, dry, less-is-more, antique leather, sturdy wood-and-brass type to take Trump's positions is that all those people agree with NPR on everything. Their good taste is their undoing.

Only someone who brags about his airline's seatbelt buckles being made of solid gold would have the balls to do what Trump is doing. Being crude is an indispensable requirement. It gives him resistance to the opinion of Manhattan sophisticates.

It's extremely rare for people to take positions that will hurt them with their friends. Being pro-choice in Hollywood: not brave. Being pro-choice in Mississippi: brave. Trump lived among fancy Manhattanites. What he was saying on immigration—to say nothing of eliminating the carried interest deduction for hedge fund managers—was going to cost him friends. Trump didn't care.

He has no nerve endings for peer pressure. The standard riposte to someone who wants to restrict immigration is: *You don't understand—your positions are very gauche, very déclassé. They're not shared by the people you want to impress. These are the opinions of ethnics in the outer boroughs.*

Other people would say, "Oh, my gosh—did anyone see?" Trump said, *Yeah, I think I still want to build a wall.*

The sophisticates didn't have a comeback. They'd never gotten that far with anyone else.

The media successfully smeared Romney as an out-of-touch multimillionaire, whacking working-class Americans with his polo mallet. He was helpless. Tasteful people don't talk about themselves, and they certainly don't talk about money. Not Trump! Early in Trump's campaign, journalist Mark Halperin asked him about the "backlash against rich candidates like Mitt Romney—any chance of that with you?" Trump said, "First of all, he wasn't rich."

And that was that. How do you attack someone for being rich who is constantly bragging about how rich he is? Yes, yes, I'm a WASP, too—it's appalling, embarrassing, awful—but oh, my gosh,

does it work! Luckily, voting machines register only *yes* or *no*—not
yes, but I hate myself.

Trump is like a Shakespearean "fool": he seems crass because
he speaks the truth. Fashionable people might cringe when Mike
Tyson shows up at the inaugural ball as a guest of honor, but nobody else is giving us a wall.

The Trump candidacy puts Democrats in an extremely awkward
position. They are the party of elegance and fabulosity, but also claim
to be the party of the "blacks and browns"—who see absolutely nothing wrong with Trump's taste. Jay Z and Beyoncé may not like
Trump's positions, but, boy, they like his style. They're asking themselves, *How can a person of such taste be a Republican?* He's P. Diddy
in the Hamptons, disturbing the neighbors with his parties.

The more you think about it, the more you realize Trump has
an awful lot of useful tools in his toolbox: he has all that on-camera
experience; he's perfectly comfortable walking into a gaggle of mi-
crophones; he loves being in the limelight and he's gotten really
good at it.

If Trump hadn't been a "narcissist"—or, as we now see it, a self-
confident alpha male—he would never have raised all those awesome issues, and certainly would have backed down at the first yelp
from the press. Americans would have had to watch in horror as
he clarified that what he *meant* was that Mexico was sending us its
David Livingstones and Niels Bohrs, to do the jobs Americans
won't do.

In Trump's first week running for president, he lost tens of mil-
lions of dollars for the "Mexican rapists" line alone. Univision
dumped Trump's Miss USA pageant; NBC dumped both the Miss
USA and Miss Universe pageants; Macy's dumped his ties; and
ESPN dumped his Trump National Golf Club for the Celebrity
Golf Classic.

Asked about the lost businesses, he said, "I had disloyal people like Macy's, and like others, 'Oh, Donald, you're a little controversial, we're going to have to drop you, we're going to have to'—I said, 'I don't care. The ties, what do they mean to me? [*Motions to the moderator*] He's wearing one of my ties, by the way, it's very nice. Very nice. I never liked them that much because they were made in China, so it never mattered that much."[13]

If it takes a narcissist to do that, we need more narcissists running for public office.

If Trump hadn't been publicity-seeking, living in the limelight his entire life, he wouldn't have been so thoroughly vetted. The tabloids had already devoted forty years to chronicling his bankruptcies, marriages, divorces—even how he was in bed (*New York Post* headline: "Best Sex I've Ever Had").

If he hadn't spent decades in the spotlight, Trump wouldn't have known to be contemptuous of the press and might have tried to be friends with them, like other Republicans. The average Republican will sell out the entire GOP just to get a little chuckle from a Charlie Rose panel.

If he hadn't been a billionaire, Trump couldn't have self-financed his run and would have had to rely on donors, who would have ruined his campaign.

If he hadn't been a reality TV star, he wouldn't be entertaining enough for tens of thousands of people to drive hundreds of miles to his rallies every week, millions to follow him on Twitter, or twenty million to tune in and watch whenever he was on a debate stage. A lot of people may have started watching him simply to be entertained, but then they'd hear what he was saying and think, *I agree with that!*

We were supposed to be appalled that Trump was an "entertainer"—considered the height of clever put-downs—but if he hadn't been part professional wrestler, he couldn't say the things he said. He was in on the joke. Audiences weren't put off when he bragged about how rich he was or how he was crushing the competition—they laughed. He was Muhammad Ali saying, "It's hard to be humble when you're as great as I am." As much as the media tried to portray Trump as a dangerous demagogue, normal people could see Trump didn't talk with a snarl, but a wink.

If he didn't torment his detractors, they would have buried him. The media were frustrated enough with the occasional Republican whose entire life does not revolve around getting fawning write-ups in the Style section of *The Washington Post*. They'd never encountered anything like Trump. He punched back.

A month after Trump announced his run, Arianna Huffington's Web site *The Huffington Post* published a "Note About Our Coverage of Donald Trump's 'Campaign,'" stating that henceforth the Web page would cover him not in its Politics section but in the Entertainment section, "next to our stories on the Kardashians and The Bachelorette."[14] The typical GOP response would have been to rise above it, to refuse to dignify the insult with a response and expect to be admired for such gallantry. (And then lose.) Trump's response was to tweet about Arianna: "I fully understand why her former husband left her for a man—he made a good decision."

Imagine Mitt Romney doing that.

Trump is a fighter and doesn't care that his blunt talk might not be everyone's cup of tea. He wasn't going to sit and listen to nonsense without saying something. At least he said things that were true.

The Trumpian skill set was illustrated in his exchange with Megyn Kelly about the "war on women." (I personally think she's right. It is well past time the GOP rethink that ill-considered war.)

KELLY: Mr. Trump, one of the things people love about you
   is you speak your mind and you don't use a politician's
   filter. However, that is not without its downsides, in

particular when it comes to women. You've called women you don't like fat pigs, dogs, slobs, and disgusting animals. [*Laughter*] Your Twitter account—

TRUMP: Only Rosie O'Donnell. [*Huge laughter*]

KELLY: No, it wasn't. For the record, it was well beyond Rosie O'Donnell.

TRUMP: Yes, I'm sure it was.

KELLY: Your Twitter account has several disparaging comments about women's looks. You once told a contestant on *Celebrity Apprentice* it would be a pretty picture to see her on her knees. Does that sound to you like the temperament of a man we should elect as president? And how will you answer the charge from Hillary Clinton, who is likely to be the Democratic nominee, that you are part of the war on women?

Inasmuch as all Republicans would soon begin to mimic Trump's response, politicians might want to print out the rest of his answer and tattoo it on their forearms:

TRUMP: I think the big problem this country has is being politically correct. I've been challenged by so many people, and I don't frankly have time for total political correctness. And to be honest with you, this country doesn't have time either. This country is in big trouble. We don't win anymore. We lose to China. We lose to Mexico, both in trade and at the border. We lose to everybody.

Not only did Trump get the biggest laugh of the night with his Rosie O'Donnell line, but his point about political correctness struck a gigantic, exposed nerve. American workers are being

replaced with foreign workers, manufacturing jobs are gone, the
rest of the world is spinning out of control, savages are chopping
off heads—not only in the Middle East but right here at home in
Oklahoma—and we need a NASDAQ ticker to know which words
have been ruled "offensive." (Would that our borders were policed
as well as our speech!)

No Republican consultant saw it coming. They had no inkling
of the pent-up rage against political correctness. To the contrary,
most Republican officeholders kept letters of resignation on file,
just in case they ever inadvertently used a phrase not approved by
the editors of *Salon*.

Not Trump. He not only took a sledgehammer to political correctness but exposed the word police as sourpuss killjoys, saying
to Megyn, "Frankly, what I say—and oftentimes it's fun, it's kid-
ding, we have a good time—what I say is what I say."

Then he sent a Trumpian warning shot across Megyn's—and
Fox News'—bow, saying, "And honestly, Megyn, if you don't like it,
I'm sorry. I've been very nice to you, although I could probably
maybe not be, based on the way you have treated me. But I wouldn't
do that." He concluded with a powerful statement, giving us a pre-
view of a Trump presidency: "But you know what, we need
strength, we need energy, we need quickness, and we need brain
in this country to turn it around. That I can tell you right now."

ROME BURNS;
INTELLECTUALS COMPLAIN ABOUT
THE GOLD FIXTURES

Conservative intellectuals reacted to Trump's candidacy with
a kind of sick horror. Among the most embarrassing objections
came from the once-respected Charles Murray, who has spent decades from his perch at the American Enterprise Institute

chronicling the fate of America's poor and working class. In a strange tirade, he announced that he was not voting for the GOP nominee—who was NOT better than Hillary!—because Trump had misstated something about the funding imperatives of Common Core. *It's WERE not "was," you ignoramus.*

It was one thing to write sensitively about America's forgotten working class, but another thing to do something about it.

The economy keeps shrinking, America produces nothing, people can't find meaningful work, and the federal budget has doubled again this year—*wow! There seems to be a kind of embezzlement or something*—but both political parties kept saying, *Trust us, blue-collar workers, give us just one more election!* What about judges? The fate of the Second Amendment hangs in the balance with this election. We have never faced a more implacable enemy at a more crucial juncture, but our intellectuals complain that Trump is tacky.

As fun as it was watching Trump refuse to genuflect to political correctness, I have yet to meet a person who says, *Well, I disagree with Trump on the issues—I just like his personality!*

It's not as if the GOP is lousy with candidates who would build a wall, bring back jobs, and avoid wars—but voters settled on the reality TV star. Whatever they thought of Trump's personal style, that just isn't how most Americans judge people, least of all presidential candidates. That's how snobs judge people. Conservative intellectuals turned out to be the most status-conscious, superficial snobs of all.

Their disdain was all about Trump's style. Regular Americans were voting on issues, and the intellectuals were voting on style.

Harry Truman was sneered at in exactly the same way, with prim matrons appalled that FDR had agreed to run with a bumpkin haberdasher from Missouri. Like Trump, Truman would make cruel jokes about his opponents, then refuse to apologize. He ended up being one of the most personally liked presidents in U.S. history.

Of course, one can't help but notice that if Trump is elected president, it will prove the utter irrelevance of Washington think tanks like Murray's AEI. Trump wasn't hatched in an incubator of great ideas. He has no use for their meaningless parlor games—retiring to the study, dismissing the women, bringing out brandy glasses, and spending all night dancing on the head of a pin.

> *Charles Murray, I believe you and Charles Krauthammer have a dispute with Charles Lane.*
> Yes, I thought Charles had a fascinating demurral, refuting in part, but not in sum, Charles's broadside against Jeffersonian progressivism . . .
> *Although I agree with what Charles said, I would distinguish myself from the other Charleses. . . .*

You know one person who was not remotely interested in Murray's erudite takedown of Trump? Kate Steinle. Also, people who can't take their kids to the San Francisco pier, who lost a leg at the Boston Marathon, and who are worried about their kids' education because we have to educate Mexico's children. Their message to the Charleses was: *Please, go f— yourselves.*

Or, for short, GO, TRUMP! He doesn't parse policy papers. He sees illegals streaming across the border and, being a construction guy, says: *Let's build a wall.* It works in Israel, it works in China, and it will sure work better than doing nothing. He doesn't need think tanks. He just needs a bunch of guys in construction.

That is antithetical to everything Charles Murray stands for. When Trump is staying at the Blair House the day before his inauguration, he won't be going to a dinner party at George Will's house, where he can meet all the Charleses and hash out issues of federalism in an administrative state. He'll be meeting with concrete and rebar guys.

We've got a country to save. No one cares if the man who will do it has been hosting reality TV shows and building golf courses. And anyway, is the presidency really that high a bar? Our current president was a community organizer, the last guy was a president's son, and the one before that was a rapist. How could Trump ever imagine that he was qualified for such an august office?

If Charles Murray is so offended by Trump's trophy wife and divorces, then how about this: produce another candidate with his positions on immigration and trade. It was beginning to seem as if no one in Washington cared about Americans.

Conservatives are not in the wilderness, this is not 1965, Goldwater didn't just lose in a landslide. Our moment is now. At every great turning point in history—Normandy, the moon landing, Reagan's election—there were always naysayers, bleating, *But what if the rocket burns up on reentry? What if the boats sink?* Today we're getting: *Yes, that is an inflection point of the* Federalist Papers *Trump has never really addressed. Everybody thank Charles for bringing it to our attention.*

It may be that Trump never wins over any swells, that Fox News and *National Review* are never reconciled to him. But ten million people who haven't voted in three decades *can't wait* to vote for Trump.

CHAPTER THREE

First Principle of the GOP: "Who Asked You?"

The Republican establishment has no idea how much ordinary voters hate both parties. If anything, they hate Republicans more. The only difference is, the GOP will lie about their intentions, whereas Democrats make perfectly clear they are the party of rich urban elites and minority grievance groups, and that they fully intend to screw over ordinary Americans.

The RNC has been forcing Republican candidates to take suicidal positions forever. Candidates agreed to bite their tongues and never mention things that are hugely popular with ordinary people but very unpopular with a teeny, tiny group of Republican donors— immigration, trade, and wars to remake the Middle East. They were happy to get 100 percent of the Business Roundtable vote and 20 percent of the regular vote. Trump's calculation is that he can sacrifice the votes of the "elites" and drive up his vote with everyone else.

The (utterly mediocre) elites sneer at Trump voters as "low-information" voters, but it turns out they were just "low-tolerance-for-establishment-BS" voters. They've been waiting forever to hear *vox clamantis in deserto*. That happened to be Donald Trump.

It was as if all the Republican candidates got together and agreed to never use steroids. No one would be at a competitive disadvantage, because none of them would have popular positions.

Then Trump came along and said, *I don't care. I'm taking steroids.* That made him much better than all the other candidates. When he didn't back down in the face of wall-to-wall hysteria, it showed his courage and toughness. His whole secret was: take popular positions!

Trump proved it's not a suicidal act to notice that high levels of immigration do not benefit most Americans. Republicans refuse to understand that not *all* rising tides lift *all* boats. There are ways the rich can do well while most of the country does worse. The globalization of our economy means that the very rich get a much bigger share of a much smaller pie. When jobs are outsourced or given to illegal aliens, the employer is better off. Mexicans are better off—they're making $3 an hour instead of $1 an hour. But most Americans are massively worse off.

Washington Republicans and their army of well-paid advisers have been completely buffaloed by the money people in the party for decades. Our elected representatives weren't even driving a tough bargain with the donor class. The super rich got tax cuts. They got Social Security privatization. They got a $700 billion TARP bailout. They've gotten trillions of dollars pumped into Wall Street by the Federal Reserve.[15]

But the plutocrats could never give us *anything* on the border.

To keep people distracted, the party obsesses over irrelevant issues—ISIS! EXIM Bank! Farm subsidies! Bonus depreciation! The death tax!—while they get on with the serious business of raising billions of dollars, siphoning off their take, and ensuring the transfer of power from their constituents to billionaires and foreigners.

ISIS sounds important because it's foreign, but it has very little impact on most Americans' lives. (For my younger readers: the Middle East has been a hellhole for a thousand years and will continue to be a hellhole for the next thousand years.) If your elected representative is talking to you about ISIS, he's planning to outsource your job and move Syrian refugees into your neighborhood.

There has probably never been such a disconnect between what regular people are concerned about and what the political class cares about.

If you had taken a hidden microphone to the bleachers at a Cubs game in 1970, there would have been a pretty close correlation between what Americans were talking about and what was being talked about on the stump. With politicians today, there's a .00000000001 correlation. With Trump, there's nearly a one-to-one correlation.

It never occurs to Washington that when the GOP wins an election, there is no corresponding "win" for the unemployed blue-collar voter in North Carolina. He still loses his job to a foreign worker or a closed manufacturing plant, his kids are still boxed out of college by affirmative action for immigrants, his community is still plagued with high taxes and high crime brought in with all that cheap foreign labor. Trump is the first opportunity voters have had to re-enfranchise themselves and disenfranchise the globalist plutocrats.

If it were anyone but Trump, he would need the party and the donors. But by self-financing his campaign, he wasn't saddled with the party calling the shots. Trump has finally freed conservatives from the Republican Party! His candidacy proves that conservative issues are a lot more popular than the party. The rallying cry of Republicans who have shrunk the party by selling out the base is: "elections are about addition not subtraction" (Karl Rove); "this should be all about addition, not subtraction," "I'm all about addition, not subtraction," "Well, again, I'm all for addition, not subtraction," and "Remember, I've said I'm for addition, not subtraction" (Dana Perino); "But look, ultimately, you know, politics is about addition, not subtraction" (Stuart Stevens); "the only way that we win is through addition, not through subtraction" (RNC Communications Director Sean Spicer); and "politics . . . is always and everywhere about addition and not subtraction" and "Politics is about addition" (Brit Hume).[16]

But Trump did addition by subtraction: he cut Washington Republicans loose and swept the primaries.

All of official Washington—the consultants, polling firms, think tanks, political committees—have been acting like they're the smart half of the team, but Trump has proved they're a bunch of impotent nose-pickers. He slaughtered his well-funded rivals with no polls, with no consultants, and with more than $75 billion in TV ads being run against him.[17] Trump was too cheap to hire any consultants. He'd do whatever he wanted to do anyway, so why pay some idiot like Stuart Stevens?

The donor class must have watched in amazement as Trump rose like a rocket by doing everything the political experts said was crazy. Donors figured the consultants must know what they're doing because they're expensive. Now they're saying, *Holy @#$%! I guess this immigration issue was bigger than we were told by Karl Rove and Mike Murphy!* Credulous billionaires are finally realizing they've been ripped off by the consultants. At least they won't have to keep giving millions of dollars to super PACs.

Maybe there are some geniuses working for the RNC, but you sure wouldn't know it from their record. The GOP had been playing a ball-control game. They were able to eke out a few victories, in spite of their Republicanness, but it was becoming increasingly clear that the policies the base supported, they were actually against, and everything the base opposed, they were for. While the voters wanted more health care and less invading of other countries, GOP elites were determined to give them less health care coverage and more invading of other countries.

Elected Republicans run for office on defending the middle class, then get to Washington and concentrate on gifts to big business. They'd say, *Of course we're with you on immigration, but unless you write us a check there's nothing we can do!* Then they get elected and say, *Oh yeah . . . about immigration, we'll be screwing you over on that—but we are going to pass a job-killing trade deal! And don't worry—Wall Street will be getting a blank check. I think a little gratitude is in order.*

That's not what we asked for!

Why don't Republicans cut campaign commercials on preserving the carried interest loophole for hedge fund managers? No, they don't like to talk about that when they're asking for our vote.

The goals the GOP purportedly sought to advance had nothing to do with the party's real goal: protecting the territorial Republican Party. With the GOP, the organization itself had become the cause—not the stated goals of the organization. Washington Republicans are like Yasser Arafat: they never seriously wanted to govern; they just want to keep their neat, static lives.

The RNC, Heritage Foundation, American Enterprise Institute, American Conservative Union, and the rest of the Brain Trust are like disease foundations. They have permanent offices, organizational structures, annual fundraisers, and twenty-fifth-anniversary galas. But we don't want a successful organization. We want to cure the disease. Our motto isn't "The Republican Party, Now and Forever." It's "The United States of America, Now and Forever."

We call it the Republican "Party," but what is that? We don't have a cotillion. We don't have sack races. All we have is a set of ideas. If the people running the party don't share those ideas, then how are they Republicans? They were publicly denouncing the nominee for the one thing a party does of consequence: push specific policies to better the lives of all Americans, not just the RNC's special friends.

YOUR COUNTRY OR YOUR RIDICULOUS SALARY?

The spineless she-males in the consulting class don't want any change in the system that's made them wealthy. They don't mind losing, as long as they win often enough to maintain the illusion that there's a two-party system.

Republican insiders treat the base like children. They have an affectionate disregard for voters, as if they were dealing with little kids who don't want to go to bed. *You'll thank me tomorrow—we need the Hispanic vote, and the donors want cheap labor.* What good stuff were they doing while working with Obama to grant millions of illegal aliens amnesty?

Supporting Trump settles the score. Trump smoked out all the cheap labor hacks on trade and immigration. What on earth was their counterargument?

> TRUMP: *We can't keep doing this to our poor and working class.*
> GOP: We don't care about our poor and working class!

How was the official Republican Party doing on returning abortion to the states? It's been nearly half a century since *Roe v. Wade,* and Republicans have made absolutely zero progress.

The Brain Trust is genuinely alarmed: *Wait a minute! You guys aren't serious about winning? That could be disruptive.* People don't like upheaval, and for the most part that's a decent instinct. But if

you want a conservative country, you need a conservative popu-
lace. Immigration is changing the country, and there will be no
changing it back. If you don't understand that, you are the enemy
of any conservative undertaking.

Trump did conservatives a huge favor by forcing Republicans
to finally admit they're for open borders and don't particularly care
what kind of country this becomes.

There's no question but that the country is heading toward being Brazil. One doesn't have to agree with the reason to see that
the very rich have gotten much richer, placing them well beyond
the concerns of ordinary people, and the middle class is disappear-
ing. America doesn't make anything anymore, except Hollywood
movies and Facebook. At the same time, we're importing a huge
peasant class, which is impoverishing what remains of the middle
class, whose taxes support cheap labor for the rich.

Washington think tanks churned out papers claiming that
dumping millions of poor people on the country is "good for the
economy." How can that possibly be good for the people who already
live here? No, it's obviously a net loss for the people already here.

> *Are you bringing food to the dinner party?*
> Even better: I'm bringing a bunch of guests!
> *No, no—we need a casserole or side dish!*
> You're not listening: I'm bringing two dozen of my friends!
> And they're not bringing anything either!

Americans aren't stupid. They can see their taxes going up, they
notice when they don't hear a word of English being spoken in their
neighborhoods, they can see that traditional celebrations are being
canceled for not being "inclusive," and they know their schools
don't have money for programs because it's all going to English-
as-a-second-language classes.

The donor class doesn't care. The rich are like locusts: once they've picked America dry, they'll move on to the next country. A hedge fund executive quoted in *The Atlantic* a few years ago said, "If the transformation of the world economy lifts four people in China and India out of poverty and into the middle class, and meanwhile [that] means one American drops out of the middle class, that's not such a bad trade."[18]

It's a real head-scratcher how Trump swept the country.

D.C.'S ARISTOCRACY: USE ANY FORK YOU LIKE, JUST SNEER AT THE RIGHT PEOPLE

Politics has created a class of people who have plenty of money, leaving them lots of leisure time to focus on status. *I've got the money; now I need to be cool.* That meets a need, but it's not the same thing as helping the country. It's social climbing.

The Republican Brain Trust is mostly composed of comfortable, well-paid mediocrities who, by getting a gig in politics, earn salaries higher than a capitalist system would ever value their talents. They were happy being the affable, loyal opposition. It was a good life being the Washington Generals to the Democrats' Harlem Globetrotters. Some of them even had the respect of Jonathan Alter! They could make incisive comments on TV, write for their little magazines, and attend conferences on the Internet tax bill or health insurance "portability"—none of which will be relevant in a country where foreigners are outvoting Americans.

They don't care. The political class's motto is: "I only regret that I have but one country to lose for my TV gig."

Washington Republicans' pathological hatred of Trump has been a real revelation. The Democratic Party became a "lifestyle" party long ago; now Republican apparatchiks are right there with them. Loyal drones for the establishment were all together in their oligarchic globalist conspiracy against Americans. At this point, Rachel Maddow and Ted Cruz could be comfortable at dinner together. Hillary and Rubio would show up in matching pantsuits as Paul Ryan and Ben Sasse adroitly refilled the water glasses.

Our political overlords say: *We don't know anyone who's lost a job over a trade deal, and besides, that's way less important than Mattress Girl.* Urban elites hear about NAFTA and say, *Yeah, that's too bad about those steelworkers in Ohio . . . BUT THERE'S A WOMAN AT A MANHATTAN LAW FIRM WHO DESERVES TO MAKE PARTNER!* They would be shocked to learn that there are millions of people in America who have no idea who Lena Dunham is.

Madeleine Albright, former secretary of state, glances out of her plane widow, sees flyover country, and thinks: *Let's put the refugees here!* For the past year Albright has repeatedly said "we" should let in more Syrian refugees, explaining, "I fly across the United States a lot. We are a very big country and there's plenty of room." *Put them someplace I don't live.*

American elites are incredibly charitable with other people's lives. And guess what? Illiterate peasants from autocratic societies, who have absolutely no idea what they're voting for, can be instructed to learn certain symbols and bloc-vote for the Democrats. Wrecking the country is coming up roses for Albright personally.

Her utterly self-interested plan to move tens of thousands of Muslim refugees to the center of the country wasn't at all controversial with our media, who completely ignored her remark the first time she made it, in September 2015. But it lit up the Internet![19] Albright apparently doesn't read blogs, because she said the exact same thing, word for word, to an audience at Syracuse University in April 2016.[20]

Republican operatives were perfectly happy to continue forever as junior partners to the left. They were all looking forward to a phony game of Bush vs. Rubio, then Bush vs. Clinton—which Bush would lose. Oh, well, life goes on. Sure, it would be nice to win elections, but if that came at the price of their six-figure salaries . . . no, thank you! So now the Republican establishment is willing to take the whole thing down.

Thanks to Trump, we're going to find out if the donors have a Republican bone in their bodies. If they end up voting for Hillary, then screw 'em. We're better off without them. But I suspect most of the plutocrats will say, *Okay, okay, you're right, we tried to trick you, but you caught us—we had a really good run for the past twenty years—now we'll let you do something to help ordinary Americans.*

HOW TO EMPTY
THE POCKETS OF THE RICH

For political consultants, Trump is their total ruination. They had lucrative livelihoods as Beltway savants. Consultants make money by persuading unsuspecting billionaires that candidates need money for TV advertising, and pocketing a cut of the haul. As long as campaigns were expensive, consultants stood to make millions. But the only reason campaigns were expensive was because of the TV advertising. Unfortunately, almost no one under sixty watches TV, and no one under fifty does.

You won't hear about that on TV. In fact, you may have noticed, if you happen to have turned on your TV this year, that it was non-stop trashing of Trump from both the left and the "right."

Political advertising is a major part of television revenue. Campaign spending on TV rose from $2.6 billion in 2008 to $3.8 billion in 2012. It is projected to reach $4.4 billion in 2016.[21] That's more than half the revenue brought in by all sports programming at the big four networks.[22] By mid-February 2016, the Republican presidential race alone had produced $156 million in TV advertising. Trump and groups that supported him had spent only $6.6 million on TV ads, about 3 percent of the total. That's why you won't see any exposés of the political consulting racket on TV: it's the same racket that pays the anchor's salary.

To the contrary, starting in January 2015, the media were bristling with stories about Jeb!'s fundraising dominance. By the first reporting period, in July 2015, Jeb!'s super PAC had raised $103 million. *The New York Times* gaped at the "financial firepower" created by "unlimited corporate and individual contributions" from "a handful of ultra-wealthy donors."[23] *The Washington Post* announced that "the financing of political campaigns has been fundamentally rewired," ominously observing that a "small cadre of super-wealthy Americans is dominating the fundraising for the 2016 Republican presidential nominating contest, doling out huge sums."[24] Ron Weiser, former RNC finance chair, told the *Post,* "No one is going to go away if they have a lot of money in their super PAC."[25]

A week after these major reports detailing the individual candidates' fundraising prowess, the *Post* ran an article dismissing Trump, titled "Summer Rerun or a Headache-Inducing New Series for GOP?"[26] In the end, only Mitt Romney was scared off by the Jeb! juggernaut. Trump had no super PACs, raised virtually no money, and ran away with the title.

Boy, were "we" wrong!

Trump is running a successful campaign not only without political consultants, but by doing the exact opposite of everything they've ever advised Republicans. It's the country or their careers. The choice is obvious. The Republican Brain Trust must root for a catastrophic loss for the GOP, to give themselves bragging rights for the next fifty years.

Trump wouldn't *have* to be the end of their careers. They could simply accept that Trump is the new paradigm and adapt, like they're always telling us to do. Naturally, it's awkward to ask people who used to make $100,000 a year to clean bathtubs for $15,000 a year. On the other hand, that's what they've asked the middle class and working class to do. Maybe wizened campaign vets could continue their "education," as Rubio advises outsourced Americans. That seems like a better strategy than being the buck-naked emperor, standing there talking about your bespoke suit.

But it's the only game they know. The mystical belief that money wins elections is how Washington power brokes hold sway over credulous billionaires and line their own pockets. They conned everyone—the donors, the media, and, most of all, themselves.

How are consultants going to shake down donors for money now? This election is existential for conservative media, consultants, pundits, and pollsters. They had to use any means at their disposal to destroy Trump—they've got lifestyles to maintain and kids in college. *You attack him for being too left-wing; I'll attack him for being too right-wing. Then we'll have a year to make people forget about it.*

In their blind hatred to save their jobs, Trump critics denounced him for having been pro-choice, then denounced him for wanting to punish women who have abortions. They were enraged that he had donated to the Clintons, which they said on a cable news network owned by a man who not only had donated to Hillary Clinton but whose newspaper had endorsed her Senate run. They were disgusted at Trump for saying some illegal aliens were rapists and calling for an immigration moratorium; and they attacked him for having criticized Romney's phrase "self-deportation" four years earlier. They complain that Trump is coarse and vulgar—and if you disagree, they'll say Trump must be paying you "for anal" or you "masturbate to anime." (That's cable news' favorite "conservative," Rick Wilson.)

To avoid hastening the ends of their careers, most of the

"conservative" punditocracy will pretend to support Trump. But they'll slow-walk their support. They'll cover him the same way *The New York Times* covered the unraveling of *Rolling Stone's* story about a gang rape at the University of Virginia. The juiciest story ever will sound like a trade report. They just need to be able to say: *We covered it!* Yes, and the best arguments will be left on the floor. People you could have counted on to run interference will sit on their hands. It will be like running a campaign with no police protection.

Trump pulled back the curtain on the whole scam. He won the Republican nomination without consultants, without a vast campaign apparatus, without pollsters, without any discernible TV advertising—and with nearly all of television news against him.

So it's all hands on deck. Nothing is off-limits and nothing is too dirty in stopping Trump. This is do-or-die for the Republican Brain Trust and the "conservative" media.

If the elites succeed in killing Trump in the general election, it will be the end of the Republican Party. Huge numbers of voters will desert the GOP for good. But if Trump wins, it will be a brand-new GOP, working for all Americans, instead of functioning as houseboys to the rich.

THE BUSH FAMILY COLLAPSES; A NATION REJOICES

To stop Trump, Republican apparatchiks will from "Republicans for Integrity," with Christie Todd Whitman, Colin Powell, and the great-nephew of some Republican like Dwight Eisenhower. Mitt Romney will show up to cut the commercial, and they'll say, *Mitt we appreciate you coming down here, but the shot—it doesn't work with that many people. We expected a bigger set, I don't know—*

something about the cameras. We really appreciate your coming, but we're just going to go with the others.

The ad will show members of Republicans for Integrity, looking directly into the camera and finishing one another's sentences:

WHITMAN: I've been a Republican all my life . . .
SOMEONE'S GREAT-NEPHEW: My earliest memory is attending the Republican National Convention that nominated my great-uncle . . .
POWELL: I've served under three Republican presidents . . .
TOGETHER: But tonight we speak as one . . .
WHITMAN: Because some things are more important than party.
POWELL: The future of our country . . .
TOGETHER: . . . *cannot be entrusted to Donald Trump.*

The New York Times will hail their courage. MSNBC will proclaim the ad a game-changer. Paul Ryan will call Trump a racist.

Let all the constipated Republicans leave the party. They're impotent, they've accomplished nothing, and they can't expect to keep getting votes from all the people they've screwed.

Asked at one of the debates if he agreed with Trump's plan to tax hedge fund managers at the same rate as the rest of us, John Kasich answered, "I don't at this point, in terms of changing the incentives for investment and risk taking." *Please donate to me, Wall Street!*

Who are all the "incentives and risk taking" supposed to help? There are no jobs! Kasich held town halls, with cooing Rockefeller Republican matrons sitting in the front rows, not realizing that after row 2, the guys sitting with crossed arms, on a break from their fertilizer plant, were saying, *You want to kill him or should I? I'll put him in a wood chipper, you pawn his shoes.*

Trump is forcing a long overdue reshuffling of the parties. The Republican Party has been dominated by the money people for too long. Bankers and corporatists, who call the shots, generally agree with the GOP on only one issue—keeping their taxes low—and spend most of their time apologizing to their friends for being Republicans. Democrats either hate the country or don't care either way, but want to win elections to save "choice." A.T.—After Trump—the Republican Party is the party of America for Americans.

At the first Republican debate, Fox News thought it would be a knife through the heart of Trump's campaign if he refused to pledge support for the eventual GOP nominee. Surely Republican voters would be repelled by a man who didn't support the party. All the other candidates took the pledge that night. Trump did a few weeks later.

But once Trump had sewn up the Republican nomination, Jeb!, his ex-president father and brother refused to support the party's nominee. On May 6, 2016, Jeb! explicitly broke his pledge—made in front of twenty million viewers—to support the nominee, in a typically boring statement on Facebook.[27]

As fabulous as it was to have a Bush-free convention, isn't it time to suspend our Homeric tradition of daily tributes to the honor and dignity of the Bush family? They have publicly left the Republican Party: Trump is the party now. These former Republicans were terrible presidents and stunningly bad communicators. They demanded unquestioning loyalty to themselves, while showing zero loyalty to anyone else (ask Scooter Libby and Katherine Harris). But the one thing we were supposed to admire about them was their good sportsmanship. Now that's gone.

In the past, whenever Republicans of conviction wavered in our enthusiasm for the excrescences the party ran for president, we were called petulant extremists. *If they don't win, they take their ball and go home.* We held our noses when they ran losers, but now that they don't care for our candidate, look who's taking the ball and going home? They don't like Trump? Good. Now they know how we felt being forced to vote for "No New Taxes" Bush 1, marble-mouthed, amnesty-supporting Bush 2, and the media's favorite Republican, John McCain. We weren't half as spiteful as they were—and we weren't ex-presidents and governors.

Everyone in the party may not share the same policy objectives, but the idea is: *Okay, this is not that important to me, but it is to you, so I'll support you and then you support me.* Instead, it turns out the moment the official GOP doesn't get everything it wants and nothing we want, they're out.

Which is more "extreme": a presidential candidate proposing to enforce laws on the books about immigration, or Republicans deciding to suspend those laws, without any discussion—and if the public disagrees with them, then they're boycotting the convention? Good riddance to them.

It's a new GOP now, remade by the voters. Who knows what could happen with a party holding popular positions!

Americans have not experienced anything like this in a very long time. Obama was personally popular, but his policies were not. He didn't ride into the White House on a groundswell of support for socialized health care. No one said, *We've got to get him into office so the Department of Justice can prosecute schools for suspending black delinquents!* What were Bush's campaign issues? Does anyone remember? Clinton's? Bush's main appeal was that he wasn't Clinton, and Clinton's selling point was that he wasn't the first President Bush.

With Trump, Americans finally have the opportunity to vote for something that's popular.

CHAPTER FOUR

Political Consultants' Three-Card Monte

It says a lot about Trump that he realized what a load of crap political consultancy, data mining, focus groups, and polling are. Opinion data collection is modern voodoo. Every company swears by it, but they might as well be reading tarot cards. That's why Hollywood studios spend $300 million on a film that makes twenty cents. Elaborate market research is what brought us New Coke.

The audience testing for *Seinfeld* was a disaster. Four hundred people watched the pilot, and "no segment of the audience was eager to watch the show again." Because of the testing, the second-highest-rated show in television history almost didn't make it to air. Years went by before any more episodes were ordered, because NBC was "afraid to go forward with something that was so strongly rejected by research."[28]

Obama didn't win because of his vaunted "data mining" operation. We were told it dwarfed any other campaign testing in history. The Obama team knew which side of the bread voters were going to butter. But in the end, he won because people just liked the cut of his jib.

Political consultants are like the biologists who cut off a frog's limbs, one by one, each time ordering it to "jump!" The frog's jumps get less impressive, until all its limbs are off and the poor little guy can't jump at all. Conclusion: removing a frog's arms and legs causes deafness.

Instead of highly skilled practitioners using proven formulas to propel their candidates to victory, political consultants are grifters ripping off campaigns and their well-heeled donors to make a pile of money for themselves. No matter how many times their formulas fail, consultants return to them, like people who remember the one time a horoscope was piercingly accurate but not the 364 times it was wrong.

The reason the 2016 Republican National Convention was in Cleveland, rather than a fun town like San Diego or Seattle, was that brain-dead RNC types think putting a convention in a state helps you carry that state. Results: the GOP didn't carry California in 1996, Pennsylvania in 2000, New York in 2004, Minnesota in 2008, or Florida in 2012. If Trump wins Ohio in 2016, it will have nothing to do with the location of the convention, but it will be taken as proof that the formula works.

Trump showed that it's issues that voters care about, not slick TV ads, clever catchphrases, or whether the convention is in their state. It's a libel of voters to say they're not issue-oriented. The only people hornswoggled by campaign gimmicks are the candidates.

Proving that political consultancy is all a con, a favorite technique is the psychological trick of establishing rapport by pretending to have a lot in common with voters. *You're from Philadelphia? I've got a sister in Philadelphia!* Or as Rubio used to say—until he got walloped by a billionaire—"I know what it's like to live paycheck to paycheck, because I grew up paycheck to paycheck. I have lived paycheck to paycheck. And people in my family still live paycheck to paycheck."[29]

There's very little evidence for the idea that voters are look-ing for a candidate who's just like them—especially voters living paycheck to paycheck. It's been proved over and over again, for example, that military service doesn't help you win the military vote. John Kerry began his convention speech by saluting and say-ing, "I'm John Kerry and I'm reporting for duty"—then lost the military vote to Bush. In fact, Obama got more of the military vote than Kerry did. Bush got more of the military vote than war hero John McCain did.[30] Even after Trump insulted McCain's military service, polls showed that the military preferred him to McCain. Contrary to the con man's spiel, voters don't expect a president to *be* them. They want candidates to respect them.

The consanguinity routines that have gotten the biggest work-out recently are: the Working Stiff, the Family Man, and the Holy Roller.

VOTE FOR ME— YOU'RE JUST LIKE MY LOSER PARENTS!

Dazzled by Clinton's amazing feat of beating Republican star George H. W. Bush—who had nearly been beaten in the New Hamp-shire primary by columnist Pat Buchanan—Republicans seem to believe that Clinton cleaned up with the working class because they could relate to his being the son of a traveling salesman. Except Clinton lost the white working-class vote.[31] The Boy from Hope/I Feel Your Pain routine was a hit only with rich urban liberals.

But we still have to hear about all the Republican candidates' fathers being bartenders, dishwashers, drunks, and mailmen—who came here "penniless with $100 sewn into his underwear."[32] Ap-parently only humble parental occupations are considered vote-magnets, because I don't remember Mitt Romney running ads about his rich father and privileged upbringing.

Asked how he would respond to Hillary Clinton when she says Republicans "support the rich," Kasich answered: "Let's start off with my father being a mailman. So I understand the concerns of all the folks across this country, some of who are having trouble, you know, making ends meet." Which means what? That Hillary Clinton would never vote for John Kasich's father? Powerful stuff, Governor!

Later in the same debate, Kasich said: "Well, Megyn, my father was a mailman. His father was a coal miner. My mother's mother could barely speak English. And their son today stands on this podium in the great state of Ohio not only as the governor, but a candidate for president of the United States." It would have been a more impressive story if there were any chance of Kasich moving off that podium.

No one looks back at Dwight Eisenhower and says, *You know what made him a great president? His father was a mailman.* (Of course, his father wasn't a mailman. He was an engineer.)

One gathers, from the frequency of its appearance, that Rubio's main campaign theme was this: "Even I, the son of a bartender and a maid, could aspire to have anything, and be anything that I was willing to work hard to achieve." *Even I, the daughter of a lawyer and a homemaker in Connecticut could aspire to be Shaft.* How are Rubio's aspirations going to help one single American?

His closing statement at the first debate began, "Thank you. You know, both of my parents were born into poor families on the island of Cuba. They came to America because it was the only place where people like them could have a chance. Here in this country, they never made it big, but the very purpose of their life was to give us the chance to do all the things they never could. My father was a bartender."

Republican debates have become versions of the Monty Python "Four Yorkshiremen" sketch, in which four members of a gentlemen's club try to one-up one another on their humble backgrounds:

> GENTLEMAN 1: House? You were lucky to live in a *house*! We used to live in one room, all hundred and twenty-six of us—no furniture, half the floor was missing, we were all huddled together in one corner for fear of falling!
>
> GENTLEMAN 2: You were lucky to have a *room*! *We* used to have to live in the corridor!
>
> GENTLEMAN 3: Ohhhh, we used to *dream* of livin' in a corridor![33]

After all the sons of mailmen and bartenders, the audience must have wanted to leap for joy when Trump gave his biography: "I built a net worth of more than ten billion dollars. I have a great, great company. I employ thousands of people. And I'm very proud of the job I did."

Trump didn't need to produce working-class family members to prove he cared about the working class. His entire platform was all about helping the working class. Whatever policy details he's changed his mind on over the past couple of decades, the one constant in Trump's life is that he likes Americans. His whole life is shot through with admiration for regular, working-class Americans.

Thirty years before running for president, when he was a young hot-shot Manhattan real estate developer, Trump saw a story on the news about Annabel Hill, whose family farm was in foreclosure. Her husband had committed suicide twenty minutes before the auction, in the desperate hope that his life insurance money would pay off the mortgage. After seeing Annabel on TV, Trump called her and promised to save the farm, pledging $20,000 of his own money to get things started.

Annabel described the phone call, saying, "If you've ever had your heart pound and pound and pound, that's what mine was doing." After she hung up, she said she thought, "This can't be true, this just can't be true." On *Good Morning America* the next day, she said she knew that "God had touched somebody's heart."

Trump called the bank to stop the sale, then went on a whirlwind media campaign to raise the rest of the money, so Annabel could keep a farm that had been in the family for generations. Within a month he had raised more than $100,000 from other big-hearted Americans. By Christmas, Annabel and her family were burning the mortgage in the lobby of Trump Tower before having Christmas dinner with the Trump family. The lovely Annabel said, "Well, we have a real celebration not only to celebrate the birth of Jesus but also to celebrate the goodness in men's hearts."

Explaining that he'd seen what was happening with American farmers, Trump said he hoped his campaign to save this one farm would "serve as a catalyst so that not only Mrs. Hill's farm can be saved but all of the other farmers, the thousands throughout the country, so that their farms can be saved also." He complained, "We give a lot of money to foreign countries that don't give a damn about us, but we don't help the American farmers."[34]

This was back in 1986. Trump has always put Americans first—typical, everyday Americans.

Two years later, when Trump was attending the 1988 Republican National Convention, he rejected CNN's Larry King's characterization of him as an "Eastern Republican" or a "Rockefeller Republican," saying that the people he does best with are "the taxi drivers and the workers."

Do you need to hear what his father did to know that Trump is going to protect the working class? That's where his heart is—and that's where his money is, too. Trump made his fortune in real estate. That can't be outsourced. He's planted his flag here. If America goes down, Trump's empire goes down.

Sarah Palin was hated for her Walmart persona. Trump is hated for wanting to protect Walmart Americans. For doing that, he faces the contempt of the high-hats. The media take pleasure in ridiculing average Americans—in TV sitcoms, cable news shows, glossy magazines, and college lectures.

Liberals are enraged by people like Ronald Reagan, Jesse Helms, and Donald Trump, who genuinely like average Americans and aren't impressed by *New York Times* editorials unleashed against them. Status-seekers can't comprehend anyone who is not consumed with the approval of the elites, much less someone, like Trump, who responds with a blowtorch.

This is why working-class Americans love Trump. They know he'll never sell them out to look sophisticated.

TELL US MORE ABOUT *YOU*

Political consultants apparently have gobs of data proving that dippy women in focus groups are *dying* to hear the candidates talk about their families. Republicans always claim they're champing at the bit to discuss "the issues," but put a microphone in front of any of them and they'll launch into an extended exegesis about their kids.

Kasich introduced himself saying, "Hello, I'm John Kasich, the governor of Ohio. Emma and Reese, my children, and Karen— love ya, girls. Thanks for watching tonight." Asked why he should be president of the United States, he answered: "Just last week, a friend asked one of my daughters, 'Do you like politics?' And my daughter said, 'No, I don't. And the reason I don't like it is because there's too much fighting, too much yelling. It's so loud, I don't like it.' You know, I turned to my friend and I said, 'You know, she's really on to something.'"

Maybe she should run for president someday. She could introduce herself by saying, "My father was a moron."

At the second debate—so we'd already met him once, and didn't care about his wife and kids the first time around—Rubio said: "My name is Marco Rubio. I'm from Florida. My wife, Jeanette, and I are the proud—we've been married seventeen years, and we're the proud parents of four children, two of who were able to join us here this evening." (The other two were in bartender school.)

In explaining why he didn't trust Trump with a nuclear arsenal, Cruz began, "You know, my daughters, Caroline and Catherine, came tonight. They're seven and five . . ."[35]

Answering a question about women in combat, Governor Chris Christie said, "Can I be really clear on this? Because I am the father of two daughters. One of them is here tonight. What my wife and I have taught our daughters right from the beginning, that their sense of self-worth, their sense of value, their sense of what they want to do with their life comes not from the outside, but comes from within."[36]

Not important, but isn't it odd that Republicans never mention sons? Do they have any?

Readers will recall that Christie's flop of a convention speech in 2012 was an extended exegesis on his genealogy: "In the automobile of life, Dad was just a passenger. Mom was the driver . . ." And it went on in that vein for another six hours.

Despite gruesome reviews, Christie must have thought the problem was that he hadn't talked *enough* about his family, and he returned to finish the job during his presidential run. His closing statement at the first debate began: "Well, thank you, Megyn. Listen, I was born into a middle-class family in New Jersey. My dad came home from serving in the Army after having lost his father, worked in the Breyers ice cream plant in Newark, New Jersey. Was the first person to graduate from college. He put himself through college at night. My mom was a secretary."

The best use of a family member by a presidential candidate was when Jeb! demanded that Trump apologize to his wife, Trump refused, and Jeb! said *Okay*. Trump had said Jeb!'s views on immigration were influenced by his Mexican wife—which happens to be exactly what Jeb! writes in the first two sentences of his book on immigration: "Immigration to me is personal. It means my wife and my family."

Nonetheless, for some unfathomable reason, Jeb! decided to demand an apology:

BUSH: To subject my wife into the middle of a raucous
    political conversation was completely inappropriate, and
    I hope you apologize for that, Donald.
TRUMP: Well, I have to tell you, I hear phenomenal things. I
    hear your wife is a lovely woman . . .
BUSH: She is. She's fantastic.
TRUMP: I don't know her, and this is a total
    mischaracterization . . .
BUSH: She is absolutely the love of my life, and she's right
    here . . .
TRUMP: Good.
BUSH: And why don't you apologize to her right now.
TRUMP: No, I won't do that, because I've said nothing wrong.
BUSH: Yeah.

Did Reagan ever invoke Nancy and the kids in presidential debates? No, he did not. If presidential elections were about who has the nicest family, it's not clear Reagan would have won.

Jimmy Carter's mention of his thirteen-year-old daughter at the 1980 debate was widely cited as the reason Carter lost. Asked about nuclear treaties at the debate, Carter said: "I had a discussion with my daughter, Amy, the other day before I came here, to ask her what the most important issue was. She said she thought nuclear weaponry and the control of nuclear arms." (Her second most important issue? Why Wendy Smith at school was so stuck up.)

Even before a single vote was cast, *The Washington Post*'s Robert Kaiser said history would record that "this was a truly grave mistake." After the election, *The New York Times* began an article on why Carter lost with this paragraph:

"Jimmy Carter almost had Leslie Fleisher's vote. Miss Fleisher, an 18-year-old college student who comes from a Democratic family, said she was ready to vote for the President until she saw his debate with Ronald Reagan last Tuesday and heard Mr. Carter mention that his 13-year-old daughter, Amy, regarded nuclear weaponry as the most important issue. Then she decided to stay home."[37] . . . Apparently, Leslie also had some problems with Chip Carter's thoughts on monetary policy.

The Republican practice of using wives and children in campaign ads began with the first President Bush, around the time the conservative movement became a fool-the-rubes marketing scheme run by political consultants. His campaign ran a slew of ads showing the presidential candidate talking about his family, children leaping into his arms, his wife and kids talking about what a good man he is, as a piano tinkles in the background.[38] It's impossible to watch without gagging. The ads have the exact same feel as the maudlin cable news montages of people hugging after some heinous tragedy like the San Bernardino shooting—which the same networks won't let us do anything to prevent.

Who are these cornball ads supposed to appeal to? It shows how little respect political consultants have for voters in general, and women in particular, that their idea of attracting the "women's vote" is to turn their candidates into Oprah. Women may like to watch Oprah; that doesn't mean they want her as president. Men like football; that doesn't mean they want William "The Refrigerator" Perry to be president.

There's no evidence that a presidential candidate's invocation of a family member has ever worked. Bush won in 1988 because (1) he was running against Michael Dukakis, who had released Willie Horton, a violent first-degree murderer, on weekend furloughs; and (2) It was Reagan's third term. Bush lost in 1992 because (1) he broke his pledge not to raise taxes; and (2) he spent all of 1992 pushing a disastrous trade deal on the country, NAFTA.

See? Those are "issues." After Bush had resoundingly proved to ordinary Americans that he did not care about their lives and their jobs, his political consultants would win them back with the piano-tinkling ads! *Didn't you hear the piano tinkling? He DOES care about people like me!*

The people in focus groups claiming they want to hear more about a candidate's family are probably the same ones who say they only watch C-SPAN, while in fact they never miss an episode of *The Real Housewives*.

But today, Republicans can't leave a stage without boring the audience with endless biographical tidbits about their tedious lives.

Instead of treacly sales pitches about his family, Trump brought back the Willie Horton–ad style of campaigning—and not a moment too soon! Liberals screamed bloody murder about the Horton ad, for the same reason they hysterically denounce Proposition 187, California's anti-illegal immigration initiative: because it worked. The Horton ad raised what we call "an issue." It showed that Michael Dukakis was the left-wing equivalent of Todd Akin. *See how badass I am? I want to give weekend passes to murderers!* (Contrary to liberal mythology, the Willie Horton commercial was the greatest campaign ad in political history. See *Godless: The Church of Liberalism,* chapter three.)

The only guy whose personal life sounds *fascinating* is Trump, and he never discusses it. He was too busy talking about building a wall, renegotiating bad trade deals, and ending our insane Muslim immigration policies.

EVANGELICAL VOTERS? SIMPLE! JUST ASK PRESIDENT HUCKABEE

Both the media and campaign consultants were absolutely certain that evangelicals would never vote for a secularist Manhattanite like Trump. Christians said: *You never asked us,* New York Times, *but we'd just like someone who doesn't aggressively undermine us.*

People in New York and Washington have very little contact with ordinary people, so they have a skewed view of the world. Whereas anyone who owns a TV set knows what goes on in New York City and Los Angeles, you could amaze elites by sitting them down and saying, "I want to show you this hidden-camera video of people at church in Kansas . . ."

Christians don't want a theocracy. They aren't like liberals, demanding that everyone enthusiastically embrace their beliefs. It's the left that won't tolerate even ineffective opposition. *Yes, you were cheering for Big Brother, but we don't think you felt it.* Feminists denounce Democratic candidates who, while supporting abortion, say they are "personally opposed."[39] Gays went to court and won the right to get married, then immediately turned to the more important battle: forcing evangelicals to bake their wedding cakes. *We left one on the battlefield—we have to go back* and *hunt him down.*

Christians aren't like that. They just want to be left alone. They don't need a candidate acting like a preacher, running around quoting scripture.

Christians knew Trump wasn't going to be siccing the ACLU on them for praying at football games or going on a witch hunt against some lone Kentucky county clerk. And he'd have a gigantic Christmas tree in the White House! Trump is certainly not repulsed by religion the way Democrats are.

At the same time, it wasn't going to be easy for the media to scare swing voters about the coming theocracy under a President Trump. I wouldn't want to be the lawyer defending the media's case on that. People are not going to stop laughing.

He loved evangelicals and they loved him, but you sure couldn't accuse Trump of pandering. His pitch to evangelicals was: "I'm Presbyterian. Can you believe it? Nobody believes I'm Presbyterian. . . . Boy, that's down the middle of the road, folks, in all fairness." In his 2012 speech to Liberty University, he praised prenuptial agreements. In 2016, he bragged about getting a better introduction than the other candidates. At least they knew he wasn't lying!

The rest of the GOP was taking no chances. Other candidates made a big point of displaying their religiosity. Shortly after announcing his run for president, Ted Cruz said, "Nothing is more important in the next eighteen months than that the body of Christ rise up."[40] Before the Florida primary, he encouraged Rubio and Kasich to drop out, saying it was time for them to "prayerfully reflect with their family." Even born-agains were thinking, *You're laying it on a little thick, Ted.*

Republicans had been getting a little too evangelical-ly lately. But at the same time, they weren't accomplishing anything Christians wanted done. How about: less talk, more action. Trump winked at Christians and said, *I don't talk about the Rapture, but you know I'm going to protect you. I'm going to do other things for you.* More than any other candidate, Trump cared about American culture not being ripped out from under us.

The GOP has gotten in the habit of viewing religion as part of its marketing scheme. Candidates preach piety—and then surrender the entire culture. Christian voters want someone who will defend their interests, not send them a thoughtful Christmas card while turning their backyard into a refugee resettlement camp.

Christian leaders like Russell Moore and Michael Gerson, who demand ostentatious displays of religiosity from politicians, have the same disease as liberals who go around being offended all the time. It's all posturing. Trump's a Christian. This is a Christian country. How about helping keep it that way?

What did evangelicals care if Trump was a billionaire living the glamorous New York City life? He was also the only person with an ounce of interest in saving the last Christian country on earth. Once the people who cling to their guns and religion aren't being outvoted by Somalis and Afghans, everything else will fall into place. Christians need a Patton, and Trump was it. Unless Trump is elected president, Republicans will never win another national election, and Christians will have to take their chances with Nancy Pelosi and a Supreme Court of nine Ruth Bader Ginsburgs.

Trump proved: you don't have to be an evangelical to win the evangelical vote; you don't have to be working-class to win the working-class vote; you don't have to have served in the military to win the military vote; you don't have to be an average American to win the average-American vote. People aren't looking for a mimic, but a champion.

VOTERS FELT FIREWORKS

Ted Cruz operative Rich Danker exposed the horror of consultant-driven campaigns in an April 2016 memo revealing that Cruz was so maniacally data-driven that he actually sent mailers to seventy-seven voters in Iowa affirming his opposition to . . . fireworks bans. The lucky seventy-seven Iowans had been micro-targeted as fireworks enthusiasts.[41]

Danker concluded that the Cruz campaign had devoted too much effort to micro-messaging vs. big messaging, arguing that Cruz should have talked more about big ideas, such as "reviving the economy and destroying ISIS." Those may sound more impressive than fireworks bans, but that still misses what Trump was doing. It wasn't the size of the message, it was *the message*: a wall, bringing manufacturing home, and an America-first foreign policy.

Trump won because he was forcing the media and politicians to talk about real problems facing the country, not recycling the same bromides the GOP has been pushing for the past thirty years. Those may be okay ideas for another time, but not when the country is about to be permanently transformed into a new country, known as "California," where all those zippy Republican ideas have less chance of becoming law than the wish list of the Wicca online community.

Americans saw that. Trump saw that. Only paid professionals whose job it is to formulate winning messages completely missed it. The vast majority of politicians wouldn't know an important idea if it landed in their laps—as it did when Donald Trump started running. They just repeat what they've heard from their consultants, and their consultants know what's important from watching cable news.

Deep in an article a week after the 9/11 attack, *The New York Times* mentioned that Mexican police had "found" thirty-three Iraqis at a Tijuana hotel, about to cross the border into the United States.[42] Except for a couple of letters to *The Denver Post,* virtually nothing was ever said about those Iraqis again. But Fox News talked a lot about the Middle East! Consultants said: *Let's ignore*

*terrorists a few yards away from our country and concentrate on
terrorists several thousand miles away.*

The candidates, not to mention their brain trusts, had no vision,
no heart, no common sense.

Trump didn't have to take polls to know what the country's
problems were. He could look around. He told us what was going
wrong and said he'd fix it.

His sweep of the primaries is a victory for issues over data, ideas
over analytics, voters over pollsters.

CHAPTER FIVE

I Don't Care What They Say, I Won't Stay in a World Without Trump

In retrospect, it's obvious that Trump killed at the debates. We've gotten so used to the rest of these plodding bores, running through all their preprogrammed, consultant-written, poll-tested talking points, that it took Trump running for president to show us what we were missing. For avoiding nails-on-a-blackboard clichés, he was accused of sounding like "your crazy uncle." To most people, he sounded like a successful businessman who wanted to fix our country.

We kept being told by the likes of Charles Krauthammer and George Will that—aside from Trump—this was the most amazing array of candidates the GOP had fielded in half a century. Senator Ben Sasse called it an "embarrassment of riches"! Krauthammer called it "the strongest field of Republican candidates in thirty-five years."[43] Will said it was "the most interesting field since the Republicans first fielded a candidate in 1856."[44]

Then we'd tune in to the debates and hear a series of increasingly heinous lines obviously written by campaign consultants:

Jeb! at the first debate: "I'm a committed, conservative reformer."

Jeb! at the second debate: We need "a disrupter to go to Washington, D.C."

Jeb! at the third debate: "We need a unifier, not a cynical divider in chief."

That's what $140 million in campaign donations buys you. Jeb! was bad in ways that aren't even logically consistent, as if his entire campaign were a bar bet: *Watch this—I'm going to run a campaign that will make voters HATE me.* He kicked off his campaign by boasting, *I'd invade Iraq!*

If some Republican wants to impress me by saying shocking things, do it on immigration. Not Jeb! He got smug and self-righteous whenever it came to enforcing immigration law. "Twelve million illegal immigrants," he said, "to send them back, 500,000 a month, is just not—not possible. And it's not embracing American values. And it would tear communities apart. And it would send a signal that we're not the kind of country that I know America is." What other laws was Jeb! flexible about enforcing?

With minor variations, all the non-Trump GOP candidates pushed the exact same issues Republicans always push: non-enforcement of our immigration laws—"That's not who we are"—combined with tax cuts, war, and hope. The main difference was that some Republicans would begin by saying, "Here's the bottom line," whereas others preferred "The fact of the matter is."

Trump was like a spring breeze compared with these clods. He not only made important points, but he talked the way a normal human being does. Even when the non-Trump candidates managed to say something that didn't make you want to hang yourself, they were largely indistinguishable from any other set of Republicans running for president in any other year. I never realized what a bunch of bores they were until Trump.

Most of the time, Republicans Who Aren't Trump were saying nothing at all. The debate format, with applauding donors in the audience, masked the tragedy of the debates. Read the transcripts for an immersion in unremitting tedium—with sporadic bursts of excitement whenever Trump spoke.

To avoid telling voters what they really planned to do—i.e., give the donors whatever they want—Republican politicians have an annoying habit of saying, "People are frustrated." They understand, they're listening—and they're not answering the question. It's as if Republican consultants all read a book on how to pick up girls and the only thing they learned was "mirroring." Candidates have learned to recite a series of facts about the topic as if that constituted a full and satisfactory answer. What would you do to create jobs? *Our economy has changed.* How would you handle ISIS? *ISIS is an organization formed in 2006 by a number of Iraqi insurgent groups* . . . What would you do about immigration? *People are frustrated!*

Mirroring is fine for the non-front-burner issues candidates are asked about—transgender bathrooms and whether they talk to God. But pointlessly reciting facts has become a vehicle for candidates to avoid telling us their positions on anything.

Marco Rubio on what he'd do for the economy: "This country is facing an economy that has been radically transformed. You know, the largest retailer in the country and the world today, Amazon, doesn't even own a single store? And these changes have been disruptive. They have changed people's lives. The jobs that once sustained our middle class, they either don't pay enough or they are gone, and we need someone that understands that as our nominee."

Rubio on how he'll help small businesses: "First of all, it begins by having leaders that recognize that the economy we live in today is dramatically different from the one we had five years ago. It's an economy that now has placed us in global competition with dozens of other countries around the world."

Rubio on immigration: "People are frustrated. This is the

most generous country in the world when it comes to immigration. There are a million people a year who legally immigrate to the United States, and people feel like we're being taken advantage of. We feel like despite our generosity, we're being taken advantage of."

Rubio on ISIS: "Well, first we need to understand who they are. ISIS is not just a jihadist group, they're an apocalyptic group. They want to trigger a showdown in a city named Dabiq between the West and themselves, which they believe will trigger the arrival of their messianic figure." (Rubio needs to understand what a border is.)

Rubio explaining why he's prepared to be president: "Here's what this election better be about: this election better be about the future, not the past. It better be about the issues our nation and the world is facing today, not simply the issues we once faced."

Republicans all got A-pluses in Characterizing the Problem class. It was in Answering the Question class where the thing fell apart. They were like the car rental company in *Seinfeld* that didn't have any cars, despite taking Jerry's reservation. Jerry explained, "You know how to *take* the reservation, you just don't know how to *hold* the reservation. And that's really the most important part of the reservation: the holding. Anybody can just take them." Anybody could state the country's problems; the most important part was coming up with solutions.

Governor Scott Walker was, for one brief, shining moment, terrific on immigration: against anchor babies, for American workers, and for a fence. And then his donors gave him a call, and suddenly he was for amnesty again. He went back to saying he was "listening."

"I actually listened to the American people. And I think people across America want a leader who's actually going to listen to them. I talked to border-state governors and other elected officials. . . . Most importantly, I listened to the people of America. I believe we need to secure the border. I've been to the border with Governor

Abbott in Texas and others, seeing the problems that they have there. There are international criminal organizations penetrating our southern-based borders, and we need to do something about it."

How about a wall?

If you really cared about immigration, jobs, trade deals, and preserving our national sovereignty, who would you put your last dollar on—blow your children away for the wrong answer: Rubio or Trump? Cruz or Trump? Hillary or Trump?

A FRESH TRUMP BREEZE

Contrast these fascinating lectures with Trump's answers. When he was mockingly challenged on his claim that he would be "the greatest jobs president God ever created," Trump didn't talk about his wife or his kids, or tell us about how Amazon does business. He said straight off: "I will tell you, I will bring jobs back from China. I will bring jobs back from Japan. I will bring jobs back from Mexico . . . [We've] lost so many businesses going to Mexico because of horrible trade deals. And now we're about to sign another trade deal, TPP, which is going to be a disaster for this country, because they don't talk about monetary manipulation. It is going to be a disaster."[45]

Instead of poll-tested catchphrases, the history of ISIS, or empathetic speeches about Americans being "frustrated," Trump had one big idea: he would put Americans first.

Three candidates were asked at the New Hampshire debate in February "what it means to be a conservative." John Kasich said, "I've cut taxes more than anybody in the country this year." Rubio said it meant three things: limited government, free enterprise, and a strong national defense. What do tax cuts or limited government do for the Disney workers who were forced to train their cheaper foreign replacements?

Trump's answer was: "I view the word 'conservative' as a derivative of the word 'conserve.' . . . We want to conserve our country. We want to save our country. And we have people that have no idea how to do that, and they are not doing it, and it's a very important word and it's something I believe in very, very strongly."

Trump, and only Trump, would put our country first and protect *our* interests when it came to immigration, foreign wars, and trade deals. He didn't care that political correctness dictates putting America's interests dead last. America for Americans.

(Author's note: After writing that sentence, I went to the kitchen for a cup of coffee, and there on C-SPAN was former first lady Laura Bush sitting with an Afghan woman at a conference of the U.S. Institute of Peace, paid for with $40 million a year by U.S. taxpayers, asking for *more* money from us for food and development in— did I mention this?—*Afghanistan*. Out-of-work American steelworkers would have to wait yet another year for the tender sympathies of Laura Bush and the U.S. government.)

Even on topics that weren't his main issues, only Trump engaged in normal human speech, free of jargon and poll-tested phrases. Someone from 1920 could have understood him.

On Obamacare:

BRET BAIER: Mr. Trump, Obamacare is one of the things you call a disaster.

TRUMP: *Complete* disaster, yes.

Then he explained the problem with health care and how to fix it, more clearly than any Heritage Foundation policy paper could. The precise problem with health care for as long as most of us have been alive is: there's no free market because you can't buy insurance across state lines. And the reason you have to buy it in the state where you live is because the left has erected these false borders so that politicians can force insurance companies to subsidize idiotic "health" conditions like gambling addiction and 180 other ridiculous things—and then shake down the people who treat gambling addictions. The only plans available are the ones approved by state insurance commissioners, who are, as Trump said, owned by the politicians. That's why your doctor has to spend all day filling out paperwork and you can't buy an insurance plan that any human might conceivably want.

Trump gave a real-world explanation of the problem, saying:

"What I'd like to see is a private system without the artificial lines around every state. I have a big company with thousands and thousands of employees, and if I'm negotiating in New York or in New Jersey or in California, I have like one bidder. Nobody can bid. You know why? Because the insurance companies are making a fortune, because they have control of the politicians—of course, with the exception of the politicians on this stage. But they have total control of the politicians. They're making a fortune. Get rid of the artificial lines and you will have yourself great plans."

Washington wonks were baffled. Trump didn't say anything about "portability" or "HIPAA." How could anyone begin to understand him if he didn't use clunky bureaucratese forced on us by government policy mavens in order to discuss the vastly complicated processes of (1) purchasing a product and (2) going to a doctor.

Anticipating the Wolf Blitzer question from the 2012 presidential campaign about whether Republicans were willing to let a hypothetical person without health insurance die in the street, Trump added, "And then we have to take care of the people that can't take care of themselves. And I will do that through a different system."

Trump was perfectly clear, but political hacks were dumbfounded. *That wasn't in my talking points!* Rand Paul promptly accused Trump of supporting a single-payer system—an incomprehensible phrase to anyone outside the Beltway. Trump said: "I'm not. I'm not—I don't think you heard me. You're having a hard time tonight."

SO SIMPLE, EVEN A FETUS COULD UNDERSTAND!

Similarly, on abortion, Trump described how he became pro-life the way a normal person might. He said: "What happened is friends of mine years ago were going to have a child, and it was going to be aborted. And it wasn't aborted. And that child today is a total superstar, a great, great child. And I saw that. And I saw other instances. And I am very, very proud to say that I am pro-life."

Isn't that how a lot of Americans came to their position on abortion? Does the pro-life movement demand anything more of a president?

At the same debate, Marco Rubio actually corrected a moderator to make absolutely clear that he did not support abortion exceptions for rape and incest. Was anyone else alive for the Todd Akin fiasco? In 2012, Akin, the GOP Senate nominee from Missouri, went from a 75 percent likely win on Intrade to 45 percent, overnight, after he said he opposed abortion in the case of rape, rambling on about what happens to a woman's body after a rape and using the phrase "legitimate rape." Any Republican candidate for president who can't learn to say, "I'm against abortion except in the case of incest, rape, and life of the mother" is too stupid to be our candidate for anything.

The Republican Party is and will always be pro-life. Who got the bright idea that our candidates should be giving detailed descriptions of how state abortion statutes should be written? Who are they, Harry Blackmun? (He's the Supreme Court justice who discovered a fully formed law on abortion lurking in the penumbras of our two-hundred-year-old Constitution.) The GOP position is: this is a state issue. In California and New York, you'll be able to abort your child up to age thirty; in Mississippi and Kansas, most abortions will probably be against the law; in other places, late-term abortions and sex-selection abortions will be against the law.

There are more than two million abortions in America every year at every stage of pregnancy, feminists are chasing babies who survive abortions around clinics to whack them with fire extinguishers, but Republicans think they have to be moral show-offs about some minuscule number of abortions that the country is nowhere close to banning.

This is no time for Republicans to be proving how absolutely 100 percent consistent they are. People live quite comfortably with inconsistencies all the time. There's no economic justification for the mortgage interest tax deduction, but we keep it because it's popular. If Paul Ryan were absolutely consistent, he'd advocate changing Medicare for current recipients, not just young people. If we were 100 percent consistent with foreign policy, there are a lot of other countries we'd be invading besides Iraq.

BIGFOOTING FOX NEWS

In addition to winning every debate on points, Trump established himself as the biggest alpha dog of all by bigfooting Rupert Murdoch and the Fox News empire. Until Trump, there was no television network, no elected official and no talk radio host more influential with Republicans than Fox.

But unlike every other Republican, Trump didn't need Fox and made it perfectly clear who was boss. They'd never encountered resistance from any Republican before, and here was Trump saying, *Screw you.*

There was no question but that Fox News was trying to take out Trump at that first debate. One of the moderators, Bret Baier, later admitted as much to *The Los Angeles Times,* saying they had even prepared a *Celebrity Apprentice*–inspired script to read before escorting Trump off the stage: "We don't want to have to escort you to the elevator outside this boardroom." They never used the script, but, Baier said, they were "locked and loaded."[46]

In addition to grilling Trump on his silly remarks made as an entertainer, Megyn Kelly asked him, "When did you actually become a Republican?" With all those hours the Fox News debate team put into their questions, they apparently hadn't turned up the fact that Trump has been a Republican at least since he attended the 1988 Republican National Convention as a guest of the first President Bush. Trump turned to the audience and said, "I don't think they like me very much."

The Fox News debate team actually spent time poring through old reality TV clips for spicy quotes from Trump but couldn't ask Senator Marco Rubio *one question* about the spectacular betrayal of voters he committed by pushing an amnesty bill through the U.S. Senate just two years earlier. Rubio had dedicated his one term in the U.S. Senate to the effort, after having run for office vowing to oppose amnesty. Isn't that more important than Trump's un-PC remarks on *The Apprentice*?

During Rubio's push for amnesty, in 2013, one of his aides famously mocked American workers for wanting jobs, deadpanning to Ryan Lizza of *The New Yorker* that not every American worker was a "star performer." Some Americans, he said, "can't cut it . . . can't do it, don't want to do it."[47] Isn't that a rather more damning quote than anything Trump might have said about various celebrities when he was a reality TV star?

This is how Fox News mercilessly grilled Rubio on amnesty at the first debate:

CHRIS WALLACE: All right, well, Senator Rubio . . . Is it as simple as: Our leaders are stupid, their leaders are smart, and all of these illegals coming over are criminals?

In what world is what Donald Trump said about someone's appearance more important to voters than the fact that Marco Rubio wants to dissolve our borders and triple legal immigration? It would be the equivalent of debate moderators in 1980 dredging up Hollywood gossip about Reagan's divorce from Jane Wyman but not asking President Carter a single question about the Iranian hostage crisis.

The issue wasn't that Trump was asked tough questions; it was that the Fox-favored, amnesty-supporting candidates weren't.

So Trump punched back—and he won. He attacked Fox star Megyn Kelly, refused to attend two Fox News debates—halving the ratings for one and leading to the cancellation of the other—and then walloped the network's designated candidate, Marco Rubio, by twenty points in his own state.

The hardest thing to notice is what the media are not telling you. Even conservatives who didn't work at Fox were so afraid of being shunned by Fox News that none of them could risk talking sense about immigration.

Well after voters had totally rejected the Bush/Ryan/Rubio/ Fox News/*WSJ*/RNC position on immigration and flocked to Trump over his promise to build a wall, *National Review*'s Rich Lowry's brave comment on Fox News was: "I wouldn't say it's unconservative to talk about building a wall. I think it's imprudent and it's—at least on the scale that Trump is talking about. And the more important issues to consider in enforcement are not quite so simplistic."

Ironically, unless we build a wall and enact Trump's other immigration policies, in about ten years, there will be absolutely no purpose to conservative news outlets like *National Review* or Fox News for insipid commentary like this.

CHAPTER SIX

You're Not Reagan

The only deep insight Republicans have had for the past three decades is: *Be Reagan!* This wouldn't be a bad plan, inasmuch as Reagan was a wildly successful president (followed by a typically incompetent Bush), except: (1) Reagan was president in the 1980s, and (2) today's Republicans don't seem to remember Reagan.

They are the political version of the cargo cult, a primitive tribe that worshiped modern technology without understanding how it worked, holding coconuts up to their ears as if they were air traffic controllers. Republicans believe they can capture Reagan's greatness by repeating his answers to the problems of three decades ago.

No voter was going to come away from a GOP debate without being absolutely convinced that these guys really, *really* liked "a governor from California."

Rand Paul at the first debate: "I'm a Reagan conservative."

John Kasich at the second debate: "Yes, he was a great one, and I learned much from watching him. The most important thing: hope to Americans, unify, lift everyone in America."

Scott Walker at the second debate: "You see, in my lifetime, the greatest president was a governor from California. Ronald Reagan knew how to go big, and go bold."

But they won't actually be like Reagan in any meaningful sense.

Reagan opposed both the media and his party to do what was best for the country. Today's Republicans dance to the tune of their donors, Fox News, and the think tanks. They live in abject terror of the media.[48]

Reagan refused to accept America's inevitable decline. Today's Republicans don't seem to notice that the country is declining, with their relentless happy talk about our best days being ahead of us— it's the new American century! All this optimism sounds delusional to Americans whose jobs have been outsourced, neighborhoods overwhelmed with immigrants, and political party has lost election after election.

Reagan was ridiculed for announcing he would solve seemingly intractable problems, specifically the Cold War. *The New York Times* complained that he was proposing "radical change" to our dealings with the Soviet Union, ignoring the consensus of "a generation, through both Democratic and Republican administrations." The best we could hope for, according to the *Times,* was a gradual arms reduction on both sides. An arms race, the *Times* said, is a war "that no one can win."[49] (For my younger readers: Reagan won the Cold War with a massive nuclear buildup.)

Today's Republicans would not consider challenging the consensus of "a generation, through both Democratic and Republican administrations," that legal and illegal immigration must continue at its current, historically high, breakneck speed. There's nothing anyone can do about it, because "that's not who we are." The best we can do is to keep repeating the mantra "America is a nation of immigrants."

Reagan aggressively opposed Republican orthodoxy on a slew of issues—SALT treaties, détente, and the Equal Rights Amendment, to name a few. Today's Republicans slavishly follow current GOP orthodoxy, like Heaven's Gate members blindly swearing allegiance to a mission they don't understand.

Reagan had a few big ideas, but famously was not a "detail man." In a book review, the *Times* said his career represented "a triumph of personality and intuition over ignorance." Today's Republicans are constantly trying to wow audiences with their mastery of arcane details, never failing to miss the big picture.

Reagan swept into office with the votes of blue-collar Democrats. Today's Republicans tell the working class they're not "star performers," their jobs are going to foreigners, and maybe they should go back to school.

No other candidate would have raised Trump's issues in a million years. How could they? There were no polls. There were no cable news "Breaking News" updates about immigration, the end of manufacturing, or whether it's America's job to turn the entire Middle East into a Jeffersonian democracy.

The paleo diet is given more time on cable news than job-killing trade deals. Immigration was raised only in order to discuss the urgent need of the GOP to win the Hispanic vote, as Republican voters are diluted with millions of new immigrants coming in every year. The only people who talk about foreign policy on TV are the ones whose relevance depends on America being at war. They'll tell us how to wage war in Libya, not whether we *should* wage war in Libya. If we're not at war, no one cares what they have to say, so they're always for war.

Trump single-handedly forced the most important issues facing the country to the center of the presidential race. For the first time, instead of the media setting the agenda, an actual candidate set it. Four years ago, the main election issues were the Middle East, Libya, the Arab Spring, Iranian mullahs, the Haqqani network, Pakistan, Afghanistan, the Taliban, China—even Tunisians got their moment in the sun. Other big issues in 2012 had been the GOP's "war on women" and Romney's beastly treatment of a classmate in middle school. For the next three years, the conservative media were consumed with the Middle East, giving us nightly ISIS updates, while the liberal media turned every black criminal shot by a cop into the next Emmett Till.

Much to its dismay, the media were suddenly being forced to discuss illegal immigration, Kate Steinle, anchor babies, lousy trade deals, both parties' defense of ridiculously low tax rates for certain billionaires, and the ultimately counterproductive military interventions under both Bush and Obama.

Isn't that what a leader is supposed to do? Trump took a gamble that if he started talking about putting this country's interests first, a lot of Americans would agree with him. He was right.

Other Republicans took a paint-by-numbers approach to being like Reagan, as if the world hadn't changed at all in the past three decades. Every Republican's three main arguments for being president are:

1. I'm optimistic!
2. We're still in the grip of the Cold War, every other country on earth is Libya, and Gaddafi just bombed a Berlin discotheque.
3. Tax cuts are the only policy that is ever necessary to create jobs and ignite a booming economy in a country that's about three years away from becoming Mexico.

For self-respect, if nothing else, Republicans have to get some new talking points.

OPTIMISM

In defiance of reality, consultants thought it would be a great idea for their candidates to be wildly optimistic, peppering their enthusiasm with lots of references to "the twenty-first century"!

Marco Rubio, a consultant-created candidate, invoked "the twenty-first century" three times in a single debate.

- "I, too, believe in curriculum reform. It is critically important in the twenty-first century."
- "We need . . . to improve higher education so that people can have access to the skills they need for twenty-first-century jobs."
- "And that's why I'm asking for your vote. So we can make America greater than it has ever been. And make this century a new American century."

You'd think the main issue dividing the GOP was whether we were in the twenty-first century or some other, less important century.

A few debates later, Rubio was giving the twenty-first century another workout.

- "This election is about the future, about what kind of country this nation is going to be in the twenty-first century. This next election is actually a generational choice. A choice about what kind of nation we will be in the twenty-first century."[50]
- "Our higher education system . . . doesn't teach twenty-first-century skills. If we do what needs to be done . . . then truly this new century can be a new American century."
- "We endeavor to do [tax reform] because we know how difficult it is for families in the twenty-first century to afford the cost of living. It is expensive to raise children in the twenty-first century."

Rubio was beginning to sound like a real estate ad.

Jeb!—another creature of the consultant class—had boatloads

of optimism and hope for the "twenty-first century"! He promised to prepare kids "to get a job in the twenty-first century." He pledged to "unite people with a hopeful, optimistic message." Not only was Jeb! hopeful himself, but he would generate hope! "That's how we're going to win. Campaigning in places to give people hope that their life is better." To really nail down his hope and optimism, Jeb! said: "Here's what I believe. I believe we're at the verge of the greatest time to be alive in this world." His closing statement was: "President Reagan believed in the future of our country, believed in its greatness, had a hopeful, optimistic message."[51]

Listeners were tense with anticipation. Did the other candidates have hope and optimism for the twenty-first century? Why, yes, they did! Kasich was alive with hope and optimism. He said, "Right now, I want to give people a sense of hope."[52] At another debate, Kasich drove the optimism point home, saying, "I've had not just a conservative message, but a positive message about how we can bring people together."[53] And at still another debate, he said, "We have a positive attitude, an optimistic approach ... You see, ladies and gentlemen, at the end of the day, I'm an optimist."[54]

Only people incapable of getting bored could have watched these debates for more than ten minutes if Trump hadn't been there.

Did Reagan ever blurt out something as insipid as "I have an optimistic message"? Instead of characterizing their messages, why don't Republicans tell us the message and let *us* decide whether to be optimistic? It was reminiscent of the first President Bush, who blurted out at a 1992 town hall, "Message: I care." Evidently, those were his stage directions, not intended to be read out loud. But today, describing your "message" to voters is considered Churchillian.

The country was falling apart, and Republicans were bubbling with optimism. Reagan was optimistic, but only *after* he'd been president. Here are some Reagan quotes from his 1980 debate with Carter:

> "I stood in the South Bronx . . . You have to see it to believe it. It looks like a bombed-out city—great gaunt skeletons of buildings, windows smashed out. Painted on one of them: 'Unkept promises;' on another, 'Despair.'"

> "We've been outnegotiated for quite a long time."

> "It take[s] more than twice as long to build a nuclear plant in the United States as it does to build one in Japan or in Western Europe."

> "The rate of black unemployment in Detroit, Michigan, is 56 percent."

> "We've endured this humiliation for just lacking one week of a year now."

> "This country doesn't have to be in the shape that it is in. We do not have to go on sharing in scarcity, with the country getting worse off, with unemployment growing."

That was what Jeb! called Reagan's "hopeful, optimistic message."[55]

At the New Hampshire debate in February 2016, after the other candidates had given closing statements pushing a "positive message" and a "hopeful, optimistic message," Trump concluded by:

1. Taking a shot at Ted Cruz for stealing Ben Carson's votes in Iowa.

2. Saying, "Our country that we love so much doesn't win anymore. We don't win with the military, we don't win on the border."

3. Mentioning the heroin epidemic sweeping through New Hampshire—one of many problems that would be solved with a wall. And concluded,

4. "If I'm elected president, we will win, and we will win, and we will win. Thank you. Thank you very much."

See? That's a message.

GOP WARMONGERS

Since Reagan, Republicans always seem to be pushing for war someplace—usually the Soviet Union, which doesn't exist anymore.

That's not Reagan—that's the liberal media's caricature of Reagan. The media feverishly portrayed Reagan as a dangerous, shoot-from-the-hip cowboy who was going to get us all blown up. Only after his tremendously successful presidency did they decide he was just a senile old man, entertaining children and telling jokes. Reagan didn't win the Cold War by passing out candy to little kids, but he also didn't win it by engaging in nonstop wars.

Contrary to what both the media and Republicans seem to think, President Reagan deployed the military only three times during his eight years in office, resulting in fewer than three hundred troop deaths. In one of the biggest disasters of his presidency, he stationed peacekeeping forces in Lebanon for two years. That ended when Muslim terrorists detonated truck bombs at the Beirut Marine barracks, killing 241 Americans. He later called the mission in Lebanon his greatest mistake. Today's Republicans strain like dogs on a leash for more such excellent adventures in the Middle East.

Reagan's other two military actions lasted between several minutes and a few weeks and cost a total of twenty-one American lives. The raid over Muammar Gaddafi's compound in Libya took twelve minutes, not counting flying time. Only two Americans died, when their plane was shot down. The invasion of Grenada, from start to finish, lasted about seven weeks and resulted in nineteen American fatalities.

In the debates, Jeb! said one of the pillars of the "Republican philosophy" was "peace through strength."[56] Wrong century. Wrong enemy. How does advanced nuclear technology stop Mohamed Atta? How does it stop Kate Steinle's killer? Jeb! might as well have invoked Andrew Jackson's warning about "unprovoked aggressions" from the Indians. Peace through strength is always a good idea—just as it's always a good idea to beware of unprovoked aggressions from Indians. But a massive nuclear arsenal is not going to keep America safe in—as Rubio would say—"the twenty-first century."

When Reagan was president, America was facing an aggressively imperialistic, nuclear-armed Soviet Union. In the six years before Reagan took office, the Soviets had extended their empire to South Vietnam, Cambodia, Laos, South Yemen, Angola, Mozambique, Ethiopia, Nicaragua, Grenada, and Afghanistan. Keeping America safe meant defeating this one superpower. It would be as if our only enemy today were Saudi Arabia.

Our current national security threat comes from millions of Islamic savages spread throughout half the globe. Americans are slaughtered not by invading Soviet troops, *Red Dawn* style, but by Islamic terrorists flying commercial airplanes into our skyscrapers, setting off bombs at the Boston Marathon, and shooting up American military bases, community centers, and gay nightclubs. Americans are raped and maimed not by the Red Army but by millions of illegal aliens waltzing across our wide-open border. Our freedoms are being taken away not by a foreign power but by our own government—in order to protect us from terrorists, international crime rings, and Mexican drug cartels.

The downside to our new enemy is: no war can defeat them. But the upside is: they have no capacity to harm a hair on any American's head, unless we let them come here. Does a candidate who calls illegal immigration an "act of love" really care about making Americans "safe"?

But most Republicans seek to prove their conservative bona fides by having an itchy trigger finger—particularly toward Russia. These days, there's no one to oppose them. The American left used to be totally fine with the Soviet Union—the gulags, the invading Eastern Europe, the show trials. Until the anti-gay stuff. Now the Russkies are walking on the fighting side of liberals!

At the debates, Kasich said, "It's time that we punched the Russians in the nose," and suggested that America go to war over the Ukraine, while simultaneously challenging Russia in Syria with a no-fly zone.

Carly Fiorina unveiled a slew of steps to stop Vladimir Putin—"Having met Vladimir Putin, I wouldn't talk to him at all." She proposed "rebuilding the Sixth Fleet," "rebuilding the missile defense program in Poland," "conduct[ing] regular, aggressive military exercises in the Baltic states," and "send[ing] a few thousand more troops into Germany."[57]

Walker said he, too, would "send weapons to Ukraine," "work with NATO to put forces on the eastern border of Poland and the Baltic nations," and "reinstate, put in place, the missile defense system that we had in Poland and in the Czech Republic."[58]

How many Americans wake up every night in a cold sweat in anguish about Ukraine? Even people afraid of global warming aren't worried about that. Ukraine was part of Russia for most of its history. It would be as if Putin sent fighter jets to force America to give Texas back to Mexico. Most Americans not only don't care if Putin takes Crimea and the Ukraine—we'd like to give him Detroit, all of Chicago except Wrigley Field, and every inch of San Francisco.

Only Trump seems to be aware that Reagan defeated the Soviet Union and that we don't need candidates playing Cold War reenactment games every four years. Trump said he'd talk to Putin. "I would get along with him, I believe—and I may be wrong, in which case I'd probably have to take a different path."[59] Not moving on from the Cold War isn't honoring Reagan's legacy; it's denying it.

Trump infuriated foreign policy mavens by asking why we're still in NATO, a Cold War military alliance intended to protect Western Europe from the Soviet Union. The Soviet Union doesn't exist anymore. (Reagan won!) The month after the Warsaw Pact was dissolved, we should have dissolved NATO. In 1951, Dwight Eisenhower said that if the U.S. were still in NATO in ten years, it would have been a failure. It's been sixty years. Who are we defending against? Is anyone worried about Russia taking over Western Europe? With all the Muslims there, Russia wouldn't want it. Republican hawks are like the gays: it's not enough to win; now we have to humiliate the Russians.

At least Republicans weren't single-mindedly focused on war with Russia. They also wanted to go to war with a rotating series of Muslim nations.

Asked what he would do about Putin, Rubio gave a little history lesson on Russia, with no clear point, but which quickly devolved into a discussion of the Middle East.[60] He perked up with detailed, but insane, plans whenever the question was actually about the Middle East. Rubio's idea was to deploy an imaginary Sunni Arab army to do the fighting for us against ISIS, despite the fact that no Arab state has shown the slightest inclination to do so.

He said, maybe four hundred times, that we need a "serious" president who can deal with the "threats we face"—which is apparently consultant-speak for importing every violent sectarian conflict in the world into our own country while starting a war with Russia just for fun. Luckily, no one asked Rubio about his last big foreign policy idea—war with Libya—which was largely responsible for creating ISIS and 100 percent responsible for all those refugees charging into Europe.

Without Trump in the race, the only way Rubio would have known about the 250 tech workers fired by Disney World and replaced by foreigners would be if it had happened at Disney World Damascus.

Kasich called for total war to defeat ISIS, with boots on the ground: "We have to go massively, like we did in the first Gulf War, where we destroyed Saddam's ability to take Kuwait. We need to have a coalition that will stand for nothing less than the total destruction of ISIS, and we have to be the leader." Incongruously, at the same debate, he said, "I don't want to be policeman of the world."[61]

If he weren't so boring, people might have noticed that Kasich is out of his mind.

A Martian watching Republican debates would think the entire globe outside the United States consisted of Russia and the Middle East and that we desperately needed to go to war in both places. Voters had to start worrying that someone would show Republicans a map and they'd find more countries to invade.

Trump was the only Republican—other than Rand Paul—who did not propose starting a slew of new wars in the Middle East. But unlike the libertarian Paul, he took an impish pleasure in Middle Easterners killing one another. "Syria's a mess," Trump said. "You look at what's going on with ISIS in there, now think of this: We're fighting ISIS. ISIS wants to fight Syria. Why are we fighting ISIS in Syria? Let them fight each other and pick up the remnants."[62] He said he'd "bomb the sh*t out of ISIS" and take their oil. This suggested an America-first foreign policy, abhorred by people who don't care for the United States but which, surprisingly, was very popular with Americans.

At the same time, all the Republicans but Trump were totally copacetic with the nonstop flow of Muslim immigrants into our country—including the more than two million we've taken in just since 9/11. Rubio dismissed as unrealistic Trump's proposed temporary ban on Muslim immigration after the terrorist attack in San Bernardino—and dozens of other domestic attacks. Instead he proposed we do something achievable, like remake the entire Middle East with wars in Iraq, Syria, Libya, Afghanistan, Yemen, and Jordan.[63]

Or we could just keep Muslims out of the United States.

TAXES

When Republicans weren't calling for war, they were invoking tax cuts as the magical cure-all for every problem. Tax cuts are great, but they don't help Americans who don't have jobs. A lot of Americans don't have jobs because Chinese and Mexicans have jobs. Others don't have jobs because tens of millions of low-skilled workers have been dumped on the country. In 1980, nearly twenty million Americans worked in manufacturing. Today, with a much larger population, only about twelve million do.[64] Politicians, consultants, lobbyists, and think tank fellows were too busy attending Be Reagan Fantasy Camp to notice what was actually going on—"in the twenty-first century."

The pundits said Trump was a "narcissist," but he may have been the only one who wasn't. Other candidates thought, *I want to be president. Now I have to hire consultants to tell me how to target voters.* Trump said, *What are the three or four things my country most needs right now?* It turns out that's the best way to target voters. His issues were the precise ones the party didn't want to face up to: immigration, trade, and war. We had just been through eight years of a Republican president followed by almost eight years of a Democratic president. It stands to reason that the nation's existing problems were the ones that neither party was interested in solving.

Even after Trump had swept away all the cheap Reagan imitations by raising issues of actual importance rather than bravely confronting the problems of thirty-five years ago, *The New York Times'* conservative columnist Ross Douthat warned conservatives that Trump did not share "the basic Reaganite vision that's dominated their party for decades."[65]

Was Reagan's "vision" to be exactly like some other Republican president? Was he great because he did everything Calvin Coolidge did, and Calvin Coolidge was great because he did everything William McKinley did? Republicans were at risk of getting stuck in an endless loop of constantly waging the Spanish-American War because that's what President McKinley did. There are a lot of qualities that go into making a successful presidency, but surely the bare minimum is that the president address the nation's current problems.

It's taken Republicans Who Aren't Trump thirty-five years to become some Frankenstein monster of Reagan. If history is a guide, in the 2046 election, Republicans will all be campaigning on the issue of who most credibly promises to build a *second* wall on our border—to fortify the Great Wall of Trump.

CHAPTER SEVEN

No Policy Specifics!

One thing you couldn't say about Trump was that you didn't know where he stood. He ran on a slew of issues that voters had been dying to talk about, but that politicians and the media refused to discuss. The media were in a bind. On one hand, they were itching to call Trump a "racist." But on the other hand, that would force them to talk about his issues—and then Trump wins.

Just trust us—it was so awful and evil, it shouldn't even be discussed. Take my word for it. Voters were prepared to hate the guy, but this was a presidential election. They needed to know what he said.

Unable to discuss the undiscussable, journalists' solution was to say that Trump had no "policy specifics," no "facts," no "nuance." When did the media ever use nuance? Journalists pretend to be serious policy wonks, but their playbook hasn't changed in three decades: *Republicans want to criminalize "choice"! They're racist! They want to impose a theocracy! They're the party of "the rich"!*

True, Trump did not have the mature, well-considered positions of old policy hands in Washington:

OBAMA, AUGUST 2012: We have been very clear to the Assad
      regime . . . that a red line for us is we start seeing a whole
      bunch of chemical weapons moving around or being
      utilized.

OBAMA, SEPTEMBER 2013: I didn't set a red line.[66]

JOHN MCCAIN, SEPTEMBER 2008: I think the fence is least
      effective.

JOHN MCCAIN, MAY 2010: Complete the danged fence![67]

HILLARY CLINTON, JULY 2004: [Marriage is] a sacred bond
      between a man and a woman.[68]

HILLARY CLINTON, MARCH 2013: LGBT Americans . . .
      deserve the rights of citizenship. That includes
      marriage.[69]

No, Trump did not have the gravitas of these experienced
statesmen, whose "policy specifics" you could count on for up to
seven seconds.

He had only pizzazz and showmanship, such as: "I will build
the greatest wall that you've ever seen," and "Donald J. Trump is
calling for a total and complete shutdown of Muslims entering the
United States until our country's representatives can figure out
what the hell is going on." How about these policy specifics: no
anchor babies, no sanctuary cities, renegotiating trade deals,
threatening China with tariffs, and making Europe pay up for
NATO? What were the other candidates' positions on these issues?

In the same breath as claiming Trump had no policies, the media would say that the public *hated* his policies. ABC News' Martha
Raddatz introduced a Trump segment in August 2015, saying that
Trump was "short on policy proposals and polarizing voters across
the spectrum."[70] If he had no policy proposals, how were they "polarizing"?

Fox News' Paul Gigot said, "Trump does not have a coherent

philosophy," and in the next sentence attacked him for being "an anti-immigration candidate."[71] Isn't being anti-immigration a philosophy? With the media, one can never tell if they are playing stupid or if they really are that stupid. (I have no position on this, which may be polarizing.)

All those angry, uneducated Trump supporters seemed to understand what his policies were. They figured it out by listening to him. It was only fair. No one listened to Trump, except the voters; and no one listened to the voters, except Trump.

Those of you who did not go deaf and dumb whenever Trump spoke might recall these policies buried in the interstices of his announcement speech. He said he would:

- Build a wall.
- "Immediately terminate President Obama's illegal executive order on immigration—immediately."
- Fully support the Second Amendment.
- End Common Core.
- Rebuild the country's infrastructure. ("Nobody can do that like me. Believe me, it will be done on time, on budget, way below cost, way below what anyone ever thought.")
- Save Medicare, Medicaid, and Social Security without cuts—"by making us rich again, by taking back all of the money that's being lost."
- Renegotiate our job-killing trade deals.
- Strengthen the military and take care of our vets.

So it was a real baffler what his policies were. What were the other candidates' positions on these issues?

JEB!: I'm gonna run hard, run with heart, and run to win.
　　(*GOP debate, August 6, 2015*)

RUBIO: Even I, the son of a bartender and a maid, could aspire to have anything, and be anything that I was willing to work hard to achieve. (*GOP debate, passim.*)

True, Trump didn't have highly detailed policy specifics like those.

Even after Trump began to release position papers loaded up with policy details, journalists and pundits agreed: *No policy specifics!* The public could not be allowed to imagine for one minute that Trump's appeal had anything to do with his issues.

Here are a few examples. You don't want to pore through forty or fifty of them, so . . . Oh, the hell with you—here are forty or fifty examples:

"The thing that makes Donald Trump so appealing is his complete lack of specifics."
   —*JOSH BARRO*, THE LAST WORD WITH LAWRENCE
   O'DONNELL, *MSNBC, August 4, 2015*

"[Trump is] running as far as I can tell a fact-free campaign."
   —*GEORGE WILL*, FOX SPECIAL REPORT, *MSNBC,*
   August 4, 2015

CNN HEADLINE, AUGUST 4, 2015:
TRUMP SURGES IN NEW POLLS

"So far, though, Donald Trump hasn't shared many specifics on his policy positions."
   —*ANDERSON COOPER*, ANDERSON COOPER 360°,
   August 5, 2015

"Trump praised universal health care in other countries, otherwise mentioning few policy specifics."
    —CARL CAMERON, FOX SPECIAL REPORT WITH BRET BAIER,
    August 7, 2015

Pushing the official Fox line, Cameron added that Rubio was dreamy: "Strong reviews for Marco Rubio, who cast himself as an upbeat, new face of conservatism."

CNN HEADLINE, AUGUST 8, 2015:
DONALD TRUMP DOMINATING GOP FIELD

"[Trump] is yet to provide policy specifics and details."
    —ERROL BARNETT, CNN NEWSROOM, *August 10, 2015*

"[Trump] is going to need to drill down and begin to answer questions."
    —DAVID GERGEN, CNN NEWSROOM, *August 10, 2015*

"Now it's time to offer some specifics."
    —SARA MURRAY, ERIN BURNETT OUTFRONT, *CNN, August 11, 2015*

CNN HEADLINE AUGUST 11, 2015:
TRUMP LEADS IN NEW POLLS FROM KEY STATES

"If you were holding out for policy specifics, you probably weren't super-excited by what Trump had to say tonight. He did not offer any new details on his plans."
    —SARA MURRAY, CNN TONIGHT, *August 11, 2015*

That night, the Internet sensation Diamond and Silk—Lynette Hardaway and Rochelle Richardson—tried to explain Trump's "policy specifics" to CNN's Don Lemon. The host was flummoxed, but Diamond and Silk understood Trump quite well. They said they supported him because of the wall and his plan to bring jobs home. It was as if they were Flemish interpreters for Lemon.

LEMON: You guys are very passionate about your feelings about Donald Trump. How did you decide that Donald Trump was your guy?

RICHARDSON: Well, basically, I looked at the TV and saw that he was going to be running for the president, and when I looked at him and I looked at his ideals, and he was talking my language pretty much—I said, "Oh, my gosh, this is going to be our next president right here." And I just felt it. I knew it. He resonated so well with me.

LEMON: Lynette.

HARDAWAY: Well, he resonated with me, too. Listen, he said he was going to secure that border and then he's going to bring jobs back to America. So that means that Americans are not only going to be surviving but they're going to be able to thrive in this country, Don. And that's what I love. He is going to make America great again.

RICHARDSON: Oh, yes, he is.

HARDAWAY: He is going to make America great. And that's why I stump for the Trump.

RICHARDSON: That's right.

HARDAWAY: You have so many things happening in our country.

RICHARDSON: Yes.

HARDAWAY: We have a border that needs to be secure.

RICHARDSON: Yes. . . .

A border? Bring jobs home? What did it all mean?
Back to the media retards:

"Obviously, that's been a big question . . . when [is] he going to get specific."

—KATE BOLDUAN, ERIN BURNETT OUTFRONT, *CNN,*

August 11, 2015

"Last night, Donald Trump was still light on policy specifics."
—SARA MURRAY, NEW DAY, *CNN, August 12, 2015*

CNN HEADLINE, AUGUST 12, 2015:
TRUMP ON THE ATTACK, SURGING IN POLLS

"The people we talked to tonight here, Kate, they say they do need specifics before they can make up their mind about Donald Trump."

—SUNLEN SERFATY, ERIN BURNETT OUTFRONT, *CNN,*

August 14, 2015

"And very important work to lay out some specific policy proposals, which we haven't seen yet. . . . In a minute: the onetime Sports Illustrated *swimsuit model who is Mrs. Donald Trump."*

—PAMELA BROWN, THE SITUATION ROOM WITH WOLF

BLITZER, *CNN, August 14, 2015*

"Now as we get, you know, further into the cycle, I think people are going to be pressing him on specifics."

—M. J. LEE, INSIDE POLITICS WITH JOHN KING, *CNN,*

August 16, 2015

CNN HEADLINE, AUGUST 17, 2015:
DONALD TRUMP LEADS IN FIRST
POST-DEBATE POLL

On August 17, Trump released his first policy paper. It was on immigration, and it was the most august political document since the Magna Carta. It explained Trump's ideas on building a wall, making Mexico pay for it, ending sanctuary cities, transferring federal money spent on immigrant youth to programs for inner-city American youth, and calling for a moratorium on all immigration. In short, it was pretty much wall-to-wall "policy specifics."

The commentariat denounced Trump's immigration policies, then quickly returned to saying he had no policies at all. It was as if JFK said we were going to the moon and the entire media shouted back, "Okay, but what's your policy on going to the moon?"

> *"[Trump] doesn't have specific answers to specific questions, and that lack of knowledge, that lack of specificity, is ultimately going to be the soft underbelly for his campaign."*
> —DOUG HEYE, ERIN BURNETT OUTFRONT, *CNN, August 18, 2015*

Five months later, Heye wrote a column titled "As a Republican Operative, Here's Why I Won't Support Trump If He Is the Nominee."[72] It wasn't about Trump's lack of "specifics."

> *"[Trump is] short on specifics. So if he actually makes a policy recommendation tonight, that will definitely be big news."*
> —BETSY WOODRUFF, ON THE RECORD WITH GRETA VAN
> SUSTEREN, *FOX NEWS, August 21, 2015*

CNN HEADLINE, AUGUST 21, 2015:
NEW POLL: TRUMP LEADING BUSH IN FLORIDA

> *"He doesn't have a set of plans. If he had to actually do the traditional thing, which is, 'Here's my policy as it relates to immigration,' his policy is not serious . . ."*
> —JEB BUSH, GOOD MORNING AMERICA, *ABC, September 3, 2015*

"The complaint, though, that [Trump] has nothing to say about policy."

> —*LAWRENCE O'DONNELL,* THE LAST WORD WITH LAWRENCE O'DONNELL, *MSNBC, September 3, 2015*

"Will we hear more specifics, more actual . . . policy from Trump?"

> —*ERICA HILL,* TODAY, *NBC, September 13, 2015*

"So will Donald Trump offer any more specifics tonight on his view of immigration? Is he prepping some actual specifics?"

> —*ALYSIN CAMEROTA,* NEW DAY, *CNN, September 16, 2015*

"I don't think you're going to see much substance coming out or policy specifics coming out from Donald Trump."

> —*MERCEDES VIANA SCHLAPP, former spokesperson for Spanish-language media for President George W. Bush,* NEW DAY, *CNN, September 16, 2015*

On September 18, 2015, Trump released his Second Amendment policy paper, which was more hard-hitting and historically accurate than the typical candidate's pronouncement on guns. Starting with the statement that the right to bear arms is "a fundamental right that belongs to all law-abiding Americans," Trump called for aggressive law enforcement against criminals and for a revamping of our mental health laws. He endorsed concealed-carry laws extending across state lines, called magazine bans "a total failure," and said bans on guns at military bases were "ridiculous." Although Trump began talking about the policy paper in his speeches, not one major newspaper reported on his Second Amendment policy paper, according to Nexis. CNN, the only television network to mention it, did so exactly twice. Instead, pundits complained that Trump had no policy specifics. His voters were just angry.

> *"[Trump's] popularity shows the Republican base doesn't seem to care about policy at all."*
>   —SAM SEDER, ALL IN WITH CHRIS HAYES, *MSNBC*,
>   September 21, 2015

> *"Look, I have a hard time saying Trump is credible on policy; but he has no interest in talking about policy."*
>   —Political scientist IAN BREMMER, THE CHARLIE ROSE SHOW,
>   PBS, September 22, 2015

I don't even know what that means, except that Bremmer did not like Trump.

CNN HEADLINE, SEPTEMBER 23, 2015: TRUMP STILL THE FRONTRUNNER

On September 28, 2015, Trump released another detailed policy paper, this time on taxes, producing a flurry of analyses either praising it (Larry Kudlow) or denouncing it (*The New Yorker*).

> *"The machismo, the bravado, the lack of policy specifics . . ."*
>   —ALEX WAGNER, ALL IN WITH CHRIS HAYES, *MSNBC*,
>   October 7, 2015

> *"It is this incredible disconnect between . . . the show that [Trump] puts on and the actual substance behind it, which I insist is still lacking."*
>   —CHUCK LANE, FOX NEWS SUNDAY WITH CHRIS WALLACE,
>   October 18, 2015

*"I'm a politico. I do this for a living every single day. I want
to know Donald Trump's plan is policy specific going forward."*
    —Fox News chief political strategist MEGHAN MCCAIN, THE
    INTELLIGENCE REPORT WITH TRISH REGAN, *FOX BUSINESS
    NETWORK, October 20, 2015*

*"I don't think [Trump has] gotten into the weeds on policy in
either of the two last debates."*
    —*ANA NAVARRO, NEW DAY, CNN, October 28, 2015*

On October 31, Trump released a blistering policy paper on the
Department of Veterans Affairs, saying 300,000 veterans had died
waiting to get care. Under his plan, veterans would be able to use
their veteran's ID card anyplace Medicare was accepted. This had
all the earmarks of what one might call a "policy."

Then, on November 10, he released his policy paper on one
of his signature issues: "Reforming the U.S.–China Trade Relationship to Make America Great Again." He began by pointing
out that—contrary to President Clinton's promises about the
benefits of China joining the World Trade Organization—America
had lost more than fifty thousand factories and millions of
jobs since that deal. Trump set forth the specific proposals he
planned to raise in future negotiations, including his demand
that China end its currency manipulation and intellectual property theft.

"[Trump] seemed to struggle with policy specifics."
    —*PETER ALEXANDER, TODAY, NBC, November 11, 2015*

**CNN HEADLINE, NOVEMBER 22, 2015:
NEW POLL TRUMP LEADS GOP FIELD
AT 32 PERCENT**

Five days after two Muslim immigrants (one of them second-generation) gunned down fourteen Americans at the Inland Regional community center in San Bernardino, California, Trump called for a temporary suspension of Muslim immigration, which is perfectly legal, 100 percent constitutional, and happens to be totally within the power of the president.[73] It's also a "policy specific."

Here was CNN's Don Lemon's probing question that night:

"Are there any policy specifics behind this that you know of?"
  —*DON LEMON,* CNN TONIGHT, *December 7, 2015.*

It got to the point that Trump could have said he was going to the bathroom and TV anchors would have complained there were no "policy specifics."

"Look, he grabs the angst of the American people about a situation and has a good sound bite, but the substance is completely devoid."
  —*KARL ROVE,* FOX NEWS SUNDAY WITH CHRIS WALLACE,
    December 13, 2015

"Donald Trump does have a test here tonight, which is whether he can actually be well versed on foreign policy, give some specifics."
  —*MAEVE RESTON, CNN national political reporter,* NEW DAY, *CNN,*
    December 15, 2015

**CNN HEADLINE, DECEMBER 15, 2015:
TRUMP HITS NEW HIGH IN NEW
NATIONAL POLLS**

"Trump understands the anger sweeping America today and is tapping into that anger. He is not really concerned that much with policy right now."

—*BILL O'REILLY,* THE O'REILLY FACTOR, *FOX NEWS,*
   December 16, 2015

THE HILL HEADLINE, JANUARY 5, 2016:
POLL: TRUMP HOLDS 17-POINT LEAD

"Trump [is anti-establishment] because of his personality . . . and Ted Cruz, because of his conservative ideas."

—*Heritage Action's MICHAEL NEEDHAM,* FOX NEWS SUNDAY,
   January 24, 2016

Luckily, Fox News has some of the brightest viewers in broadcast news. *Fox News Sunday* host Chris Wallace thought one viewer comment was especially clever: "We got this tweeted out to us by a fellow, or a woman, I suppose, by the name Steelers Slob, who tweets this: 'Are Donald Trump and Ted Cruz going to feel silly after they're done tearing each other apart and Rubio eats their lunch?'" That was on the eve of the Iowa and New Hampshire primary contests—won by Cruz and Trump, while Rubio came in third and fifth, respectively. Excellent choice of viewer comments, Chris.

CNN HEADLINE, JANUARY 26, 2016:
TRUMP SOARS IN POLLS

"The absence of Trump [at the debate] is . . . a very big opportunity . . . for [Ted Cruz and Marco Rubio] to actually talk about policy."

—*CARL CAMERON, Fox chief political correspondent,* THE KELLY
   FILE, *FOX NEWS, January 27, 2016*

"I really don't think [Trump] added much of substance."
    —*RAND PAUL*, THE KELLY FILE, *FOX NEWS, January 27, 2016*

*"[Trump] hasn't studied policy . . . I wouldn't take him
seriously enough to even try to debate policy with him."*
    —*STUART STEVENS*, THE LAST WORD WITH LAWRENCE
        O'DONNELL, *MSNBC, February 2, 2016*

CNN HEADLINE, FEBRUARY 7, 2016: TRUMP'S NEW HAMPSHIRE LEAD GROWS

*"Trying to figure out exactly what [Trump] means to do or
how he means to implement some of the policy statements that
he's made is really beyond me. I don't really—I can't really
answer what specifics he intends."*
    —*ANDREW SMITH, political science professor, University of New
        Hampshire, AUSTRALIAN BROADCASTING CORPORATION,
        February 10, 2016*

FOX NEWS HEADLINE, FEBRUARY 26, 2016: SOME BELIEVE SENATOR RUBIO WON THE DEBATE LAST NIGHT

That's pretty sad when the best even Fox could come up with was "some believe" golden boy Rubio had won. *Some believe* if you swallow a watermelon seed, a watermelon will grow in your stomach!

On March 2, 2016, Trump released his seven-point health care reform policy paper. After repealing Obamacare—step one—the single most important reform was this: allowing Americans to buy health insurance across state lines and ending the monopoly of corrupt state insurance commissions.

"[There's a] lack of any policy vision, real policy vision, that Donald Trump has offered."
  —Rubio adviser *LANHEE CHEN*, BLOOMBERG SURVEILLANCE,
    March 2, 2016

Incidentally, can you think of a worse item to have on your résumé than "Rubio adviser"? How about "Fire marshal, *The Hindenburg*"?

"Donald Trump, sadly, hasn't taken the time to learn much depth on most of these issues."
  —Former Minnesota governor *TIM PAWLENTY*, MORNING
    EDITION, *NPR*, March 3, 2016

CNN HEADLINE, MARCH 9, 2016:
TRUMP LEADING POLLS IN FLORIDA

"I tried to engage Mr. Trump and ask him some serious policy questions . . . but he didn't want to answer any policy questions that I asked him."
  —Senator *BEN SASSE*, THE O'REILLY FACTOR, *FOX NEWS*,
    March 17, 2016

Sasse claimed to have asked these probing questions on Twitter, but no such questions exist in Sasse's Twitter feed.

Although Trump had already explained how he would make Mexico pay for the wall in his very first policy paper, the American press corps were stumped by the idea. Perhaps they were unable to find that policy paper on his Web site, which apparently requires having access to a computer and the Internet. To help them out, on April 5, 2016, Trump released a bonus policy paper (policy paper number six, if you're keeping score) on a single topic: how he'd make Mexico pay for the wall.

As he'd already explained, he would ask for a one-time payment, and if Mexico refused, he had a series of countermeasures, which were entirely within the prerogative of the executive branch. Citing facts and figures—even regulation numbers!—he proposed to cancel visas, impose tariffs on Mexican imports, and block remittances from Mexican migrants back to their home country. Every year, these remittances transfer more than $20 billion out of the American economy and into the Mexican economy—mostly into the pocket of Carlos Slim, *The New York Times'* sugar daddy, often billed as the world's richest man.

This was the second time Trump had presented the media with a lengthy, detailed set of blueprints. In response the media said, *Can't you be more specific?*

> *"He doesn't have policies. He's made this into more or less a referendum on himself as a TV star."*
>> —*TOM NICHOLS, professor of national security affairs at the U.S. Naval War College,* THE LAST WORD WITH LAWRENCE O'DONNELL, *MSNBC, April 27, 2016*

CNN HEADLINE, APRIL 27, 2016:
RESULTS OF TUESDAY'S PRIMARIES:
TRUMP WINS ALL FIVE STATES

> *"Oh, policy ideas—Trump loves those."*
>> —*JOSH BARRO (@jbarro), Twitter, May 12, 2016*

> *"[Trump's] policy is just like whatever he grabs out of the air that's floating around him. . . . If you try to keep it based on his policies, which he doesn't even understand, let alone necessarily believe in, I think you kind of miss the point."*
>> —*RACHEL MADDOW,* LATE NIGHT WITH SETH MEYERS, *May 12, 2016*

What "specifics" did the media want exactly? FDR didn't need to know how to change the oil on a landing craft vehicle to win a war with Nazi Germany. Voters aren't interested in that level of detail; they want to know if a politician is going in their direction.

It would be as if we were dying to go to Milwaukee. We pack our bologna sandwiches, go to the Greyhound terminal, pay our fare, and walk to the line of buses. *San Francisco*—Nope! *St. Louis*—Nope! *The Grand Tetons*—Nope! *Milwaukee*—That's us! We ask the driver if the bus is going to Milwaukee and he says yes, so we get on board. The doors close, and just as the bus is taking off—the driver announces that we're headed to Austin, Texas.

We curse, ride the bus for three days, get out in Austin, and look for another bus to Milwaukee. We pay the fare, find the signs, ask the driver where he's going—Milwaukee!—and as soon as we're in our seats and the doors are locked, the driver tells us the bus is going to Atlantic City.

After this happens a dozen more times and we've been all over the country, we're bleary-eyed, sleepless, and frustrated. We get on another bus, it takes off, and this time the driver turns around and . . . it's Donald Trump! He tells us, *We're going to Milwaukee*. We don't care what route he's taking. We don't care if he sticks to interstate highways or prefers the back roads. We don't care if he keeps the air-conditioning too hot or too cold. We just want to go to Milwaukee. As long as we finally have a guy who's going to take us where we want to go, WE DON'T CARE ABOUT THE DETAILS.

There is a difference between the destination and the route. The only "policy specifics" voters need are: Trump's going to do it, and the others won't. He has the wherewithal to get it done, and the others don't. He's telling us the truth, and the others aren't.

CHAPTER EIGHT

Trump Hits Back

If Trump accomplishes nothing else, by the end of this, when the tide recedes, he will have validated scoffing at political correctness and enlarged the space of what can be discussed.

Political correctness gives dour, boring people a sense of nobility. Teenagers go to worthless colleges and learn the craft of being a member of the thought police. It's like the subway ads: *Yes, YOU can be an uninteresting person! Take a six-week course and make a good living as a PC enforcer!*

I think I've got it, let me try—"That's sexist."
YES! YES!

Do they really care so much? And if so, why? Political correctness was designed to make idiots without original thoughts feel valued and important.

The PC regime wasn't installed until after Reagan. Sometime since then we became a society that rewards people for being little Nazi block watchers. Apart from the fact that PC is annoying, it's now bled into how America conceives of itself, influencing public policy. Political correctness instructs that the historic American nation is guilty of everything and the third world hordes over-whelming us are innocent little lambs.

Less than a week after the 9/11 attack, President Bush gave a speech to the Islamic Center of Washington, D.C., citing the "elo-quent" Koran and saying, "The face of terror is not the true faith of Islam. That's not what Islam is all about. Islam is peace." What more would Al Gore have done?

No one has ever challenged the PC regime like Trump. He is the athlete in the Apple commercial throwing a sledgehammer through Big Brother's telescreen. He doesn't observe political cor-rectness about *anything*. He's not PC on the things that upset mil-lennial social justice warriors, and he's not PC on the cornball religious stuff—upsetting show-off Christians like George W. Bush's religion adviser, Michael Gerson, who considers himself the last word in piety. (Apparently, destroying the only Christian coun-try on earth by dissolving our borders is ultra pious.)

Any other Republican would be surrounded by advisers afraid to mention Monica Lewinsky or Juanita Broaddrick. They wouldn't touch the tape of Hillary laughing about the violent child rapist she got off by smearing the victim as a delusional flirt.

Trump ain't scared of sh*t. Hillary wants to talk about the "war on women"? *Excuse me, I have a tape I'd like to play.*

Bernie Sanders did nothing to reduce Hillary's standing in the polls. His big contribution was to say: "The American people are sick and tired of hearing about your damn e-mails!" It was Trump who destroyed Hillary, allowing Bernie to skate in. There's a rea-son the left won't call Trump out on global warming, their core religious philosophy. If they let him loose on climate change, he'd destroy that, too.

While the left's cultural warriors were busily instructing Americans not to say words like "female" and "prisoner," Trump hit them with "schlonged." Talking about Hillary's 2008 run, he said, "She got schlonged." That led to a media frenzy over the meaning of the word "schlonged" and whether Trump had used an outrageous vulgarity. Hillary ally David Brock claimed Trump's remark was both sexist *and* racist, because it implied that a black man had RAPED Hillary.[74]

(David aced his college exam in Political Correctness!)

Trump went merrily on, demanding an apology from Hillary for saying ISIS was using tapes of his speeches as "recruitment videos." This had been proved false, even by the media's standards, so the news quickly moved to Hillary's refusal to apologize to him—and "schlonged" made a daring escape into the world from the word police.

After hitting Hillary on her e-mails, Trump accused her of enabling her sex abuser husband by smearing a string of his conquests, successful and not. Just as millennials on her campaign had gotten up to speed on Juanita Broaddrick, Kathleen Willey, Monica Lewinsky—and several dozen cocktail waitresses along the interstate corridor between Little Rock and Washington—Trump hit Hillary with Vince Foster. The twenty-year-olds said: *WHO'S VINCE FOSTER?*

The whole strategy of D-Day was to trick Hitler into defending the entire French coast to catch him unprepared for the landing at Normandy. That's what Trump was doing with Hillary, landing blow after blow so her campaign would never know what was coming next.

Republican consultants rushed to MSNBC to announce that Trump's strategy against Hillary *would not work.* Polling wizard Rick Wilson told MSNBC's Chris Hayes that he'd done testing, polls, analytics, and focus groups, and guess what? Attacking Hillary just made people like her! Focus groups "hated" the attacks, he said. "They had a directly opposite response to what you would think."[75]

Luckily, Trump wasn't using any GOP consultants.

The rule that it's not presidential to hit someone was written by people who aren't good at hitting. For the past forty years, Democrats have been Justin Bieber—immature little jerks with big mouths who start fights knowing that an army of behemoth bodyguards will finish the job for them. The media are the bodyguards for Democrats—and also for Republicans who attack a more conservative Republican. That's why Republicans hit Republicans to their right harder than they ever hit Democrats.

No one had ever experienced anything like Trump before. It's like starting a fight with Mike Tyson in his prime. In the end, you and your bodyguards get beat up.

Trump is the master of one-punch knockout. The key to his attacks, mystifying his rivals, was that they were always based in truth. Jeb! was a soft-spoken beta male with no zip—"low energy." Ben Carson was even more low energy, so Trump pretended to be a newscaster reporting: "Donald Trump has fallen to second place in Iowa behind Ben Carson. We informed Ben—but he was sleeping." Marco Rubio looked like he was running for student council—he was "Little Marco." Carly Fiorina was a sourpuss, so Trump said, "Look at that face. Would anyone vote for that?"

His main arguments, of course, were on policy, repeatedly slamming Jeb!, for example, on immigration, Common Core, and women's health. In October 2015, Trump tweeted, "Remember that Carson, Bush and Rubio are VERY weak on illegal immigration. They will do NOTHING to stop it. Our country will be overrun!" But he'd also zero in on his opponents' personalities, stature, big ears, facial expressions, or other distinctive features—horrifying the guardians of good taste in the press. Is that a civil rights issue now? Somebody tell the media—they've been attacking conservatives for personal attributes forever. Anyone remember Sarah Palin?

In contrast to his own jabs, which always began with a true

premise, the attacks on Trump were just long, angry insults, like a John Oliver show. As Rubio found out (and John Oliver still hasn't), comedy isn't as easy as it looks. After Trump crushed him in the first three primaries, Rubio finally took all the free advice being dispensed from every media outlet and tried to be Trumpian.

CNN presented their dueling insults one day back to back.

> TRUMP: I saw with Rubio, I saw—and he's a nervous wreck, because here's a guy, no, he's a nervous basket case. Here's a guy, you had to see him, wait, you had to see him backstage—he was putting on makeup with a trowel. No, I don't want to say that. I will not say that he was trying to cover up his ears. I will not say that. No, he was just trying to cover up—he was just trying to cover up the sweat that pours off. Did you ever see a guy sweat like this?

If Trump had ended with Rubio "putting on makeup with a trowel," it would have been insulting, but it wouldn't have been funny. All the candidates wear makeup at the debates—that's generic. Trump zeroed in on odd traits specific to Rubio—he looked fourteen, sweated like a rabies victim, and had unusually large ears.

> RUBIO: [Trump] called me Mr. Meltdown. Let me tell you something. Last night in the debate, during one of the breaks, two of the breaks, he went backstage. He was having a meltdown. First, he had this little makeup thing applying like makeup around his mustache because he had one of those sweat mustaches. Then he asked for a full-length mirror. I don't know why, because the podium goes up to here, but he wanted a full-length mirror. Maybe to make sure his pants weren't wet, I don't know.

Terrible. Doesn't land. No one thought Trump looked nervous. These are just standard insults that any candidate could make about any other candidate.

The media's exuberant cheerleading for Rubio made his attacks even sadder. On *Meet the Press,* Erick Erickson said Rubio was showing he could be the "the alpha dog."[76] Ari Fleischer also described Rubio as "the alpha male who is capable of taking on Donald Trump." Rich Lowry said, "This is Marco Rubio's attempt to give Trump some of his own medicine and beat him at his own game."[77] Fox News political strategist Guy Benson explained that Rubio was "saying, like, all right, if that's the appetite out there in the media, we can play into that as well."[78]

Except "we" couldn't play it as well. In another by-the-numbers attack, Rubio implied Trump had a small penis with the hackiest of all clichés. It was worse than "Size matters," worse than "Too much information," worse than "Keep it classy." Like a half-bright on some cable TV show who thinks he's being terribly witty, Rubio said Trump had small hands and . . . flicking of lights, trumpets blaring, curtains rise, 5, 4, 3, 2 . . . "you know what they say about men with small hands."

At the next debate, Trump responded: "I have to say this: he hit my hands. Nobody has ever hit my hands. I've never heard of this one. Look at those hands. Are they small hands? And he referred to my hands, if they're small, something else must be small. I guarantee you there's no problem. I guarantee you."

Some Trump fans thought that was unnecessary. But you know what? Nobody talked about his hands again.

Trump's insults made him the only non-sexist, non-racist, non-discriminator in the country. He'd attack a woman for her looks exactly as he would a man. He ridiculed his rivals and members of the press absolutely without regard to race, ethnicity, or physical handicap. It was as if Trump had attained some sort of Platonic ideal of non-discrimination. One got the sense that he would appoint a lesbian Hindu to be secretary of the Army if she was the best person for the job, but he also wouldn't care if he ended up with a cabinet of all white men if *they* were the best people for the job.

Despite investigations into Trump's alleged sexism more thorough than the FBI's investigation of Omar Mateen, involving interviews with dozens of women, the media kept turning in C-minus reports that read like slipshod term papers written hastily at the last minute. You'd finish them and think, *This is not your best work, New York Times; we know you can do better.* The media were left sputtering vague allegations about Trump's retrograde attitude toward women. Even if that were true, it just reminded voters of an earlier, simpler America—an America without transgender bathrooms and petulant girls on the Supreme Court.

Trump wasn't bullying his antagonists on behalf of himself; he was bullying them in defense of his movement. He protected his supporters—good Americans who had been mocked by the media for a very long time. Trump targets the powerful. The media target the average American and everything he cares about.

When sweet, decent Americans said at John McCain's 2008 town halls that they were "scared" of Obama or that they thought he was an "Arab," McCain decided to impress the media by sanctimoniously instructing them, "No, no, he's a decent American," and, "No, ma'am, he's not an Arab." Those clips got played over and over, so the smart set could laugh at rubes being coached in tolerance by John McCain. How about the media show us the tape of the black congressman asking a U.S. general if the island of Guam would tip over if we sent more troops? How about any tape of Senator Patty Murray talking?

Unlike the usual media suck-ups, Trump stood with his supporters. When violent protesters began invading Trump's rallies, throwing punches, he didn't try to win plaudits from the media by criticizing those in his crowd who fought back. Asked about one heckler who got punched, Trump said, "Maybe he *should* have been roughed up, because it was absolutely disgusting what he was doing."

What do the media expect American men of vigor to do when thugs invade their nice friendly rallies? Dive under their chairs? Forget Iwo Jima if we don't have a few of these brave men.

People had driven hours to hear Trump speak and then would have to wait patiently for security to remove screaming protesters, one by one. After sitting through ten minutes of one screeching agitator being ejected, another loud-mouthed jerk would start yelling in a different part of the stadium. TV reports couldn't convey the obnoxiousness of hecklers even if they tried—and they weren't trying. People might see six seconds of some nut yelling at a Trump rally. For the true experience, viewers needed to be tied to chairs and forced to listen to six minutes of it.

That's not free speech; it's shutting down someone else's speech. Every live TV show has security for that reason. Try heckling at an opera performance or going to a Hillary rally and repeatedly shouting, "FOUR KILLED IN BENGHAZI!"

But the media would frame these mob attacks on Trump rallies as errors on both sides, saying his rallies were "marred by violence" or reporting "clashes" between protesters and supporters. It's like describing the Holocaust as a time when Jews and Nazis were constantly fighting, not trying to get along.

In fact, if we could find one hundred distinguished people who died fifty years ago, bring them back through the fog of history to present-day America, set them loose, and tell them there's been a revival of Nazism someplace in America, please find it and report back, one hundred out of a hundred would find parallels to *Kristallnacht* in cheerful Trump supporters being set upon and beaten up

as they walked to their cars after a rally, with the full encourage-
ment of the media and the San Jose mayor and police chief.

This is how ABC's George Stephanopoulos reported on Trump
supporters being chased and beaten by Mexican flag-waving mobs:
"This week, fists flew in the streets of San Jose, and Donald Trump
combative as ever." The fists weren't attached to human beings;
these were just atmospheric conditions.

The Wall Street Journal put the blame for the protests squarely
on Trump for disagreeing with the editorial page of *The Wall Street
Journal* on the importance of open borders to billionaire globalists:
"With his unrestrained rhetoric about Mexicans, Muslims and
even his fellow Republicans, Donald Trump has become a polarizing political figure of the kind the U.S. hasn't seen in many
years. It's no surprise, then, that Mr. Trump has inspired a political
counter-reaction."[79]

Between shout-outs to various actresses, MSNBC's Lawrence
O'Donnell blamed Trump, saying that violent protests occurred
only at Trump rallies. Duh. That's where the people are. Why
would you disrupt another candidate's meeting with a hundred
people? It's not worth the taxi fare. The only reason there weren't
constant protests at Bernie Sanders's rallies was that conservatives
don't do this—though Sanders was disrupted by a couple of Black
Lives Matter protesters once. They drove Bernie off the stage, making him look very masculine.

In 2004, Al Franken tackled a guy heckling Howard Dean. I
don't remember any headlines saying, "Left-Winger Violently Attacks Man Exercising Free Speech." It was more like "Badass Co-
median Takes Down Dickweed Protester." When Al Sharpton
spoke during the Crown Heights unrest and Central Park rape
trial, members of the press got punched by his supporters.[80] And
robbed. And their cameras smashed. Maybe O'Donnell could have
a word with his MSNBC colleague about that sometime.

The media said the people attending Trump's rallies were angry, but they weren't angry when they went in. They became angry when the events were disrupted.

Trump gave voice to their frustration, saying things like, "If you see somebody getting ready to throw a tomato, knock the crap out of them, would you? Seriously. Okay? Just knock the hell—I promise you, I will pay for the legal fees." And "I'd like to punch him in the face, I'll tell you."

As guards removed a heckler from a Trump rally in Burlington, Vermont, Trump said, "Get him outta here! Don't give him his coat. Don't give him his coat. Keep his coat. Confiscate his coat. You know, it's about ten degrees below zero outside. No, you can keep his coat. Tell him we'll send it to him in a couple of weeks."

Far from "inciting" his supporters, they'd laugh. Inasmuch as only one supporter ever cold-cocked a protester, it seemed to work.

NBC's Chuck Todd recalled the good old days when Republican candidates would embarrass their supporters for the amusement of the press, advising Trump to be more like . . . John McCain! Trump could "set a different tone," Todd said. "He's going to have to have a moment where he does that, like John McCain did. It helped McCain. I actually think it would politically help Trump if he did it. That's the irony here: it would be in his political best interest to do this."[81] How did it help McCain? He won the respect of people who hate Republicans' guts and then lost the election. I bet the media would like Trump to be more like McCain.

It would have been so easy for Trump to be praised by the media if only he'd followed the McCain example and lectured his supporters instead of laughing with them about the jackass protesters and lying media.

Instead, he attacked McCain for getting captured in Vietnam. And Trump didn't lose a sliver of support for doing it. For people who hadn't bought their Trump apps yet and were still using old measuring sticks to gauge political speech—something like an abacus—Trump's remark about McCain seemed like a mistake at the time. Over and over again, the media played Trump saying of the man who had been shot down over Vietnam, "He's a war hero because he was captured. I like people that weren't captured."

To understand Trump's attack on McCain, we first have to review the decades of mocking contempt heaped on any American who was not doing cartwheels over illegal immigration. McCain had just called them "crazies." That's why Trump struck.

Americans who lived near our border were being murdered, shot, and raped, their livestock slaughtered, their homes broken into, and their property destroyed. Washington's response was to keep trying to pass an amnesty bill. Obama came into office and announced that he would not enforce federal immigration law, which had barely been enforced under the previous president.

The state that was ground zero for illegal immigration, Arizona, passed a law in 2010 allowing local law enforcement to ask about the legal status of probable illegal aliens they arrested. The elites attacked, calling the good people of Arizona "un-American," "racist," and "fascist."

The law was slimed as the "papers, please" law, as if it were some sort of Nazi tactic to ask immigrants to carry their immigration documents. If so, we'd been living in Nazi Germany since 1940, when the federal government first made it a crime for aliens not to have their immigration papers on them.

The New York Times told egregious lies about the law in an editorial, claiming it "requires police officers to stop and question anyone who looks like an illegal immigrant."[82] *Times* columnist Linda Greenhouse wrote that the Arizona law created "a new crime of breathing while undocumented."[83] *The Washington Post*'s Dana Milbank said that "the Arizona abomination" showed that the country was "turning into a nation of vigilantes suspicious of anybody with dark skin."[84]

Obama claimed the Arizona law would result in American citizens of Hispanic extraction being "harassed" when they take their kids out to get ice cream.[85] Which was true—if they robbed a bank on the way. On *Saturday Night Live,* the perfect weather vane of approved liberal opinion, Seth Meyers said, "Could we all agree that there's nothing more Nazi than saying, 'Show me your papers?' . . . So heads up, Arizona: that's fascism. I know, I know, it's a *dry* fascism, but it's still fascism."[86]

The people of Arizona were smeared not only by these organs of approved opinion but by Republicans—the usual suspects, mostly veterans of the wildly popular Bush administration. (Not McCain, but only because he was up for election that year in the state that had passed the law.)

Bush's deputy chief of staff and corporate flunky Karl Rove told a group of Republicans that he "wished they hadn't passed it," predicting "constitutional problems." Bush press secretary Dana Perino said that allowing "police to stop people on the streets and demand their papers"—which the law did not allow—was "a bridge too far."[87] Bush speechwriter Michael Gerson wrote a *Washington Post* column, prissily saying of the law, "Americans are not accustomed to the command 'Your papers, please,' however politely delivered."[88]

This is a common misunderstanding in Washington, but illegal aliens are not "Americans."

Despite Senator Lindsey Graham's considered legal opinion that the law was "unconstitutional,"[89] the Supreme Court found the "papers, please" law perfectly constitutional. It's working beautifully, and no one's civil rights have been trampled.

Flash-forward to July 2015: a few weeks after Trump had launched his campaign with a speech about illegal alien rapists and drug dealers, fifteen thousand Arizonans turned out to see him at his first rally.

During the rally, Trump turned the microphone over to Jamiel

Shaw Sr., whose seventeen-year-old son, a high school football star, had been murdered by an illegal alien. His son was in the process of being recruited by Stanford University when he was gunned down by Mexican gang members, close enough to home that his father heard the shot that killed him. Mr. Shaw told the Arizonans that he saw Trump "as a father figure" despite their being about the same age. "He's the kind of man you would want to be your dad," Shaw continued. "He's a nice guy. He put himself out there for black people. I know I can trust him."[90]

The very next day, McCain rushed to *The New Yorker* to assail Trump for firing up the "crazies" in Arizona. To a deeply sympathetic liberal reporter, he said, "We have a very extreme element within our Republican Party" (probably the kind of people who don't think illegals are "Americans"). Just as the party was getting these nuts under control, McCain carped, Trump had "galvanized them"—he "got them activated."[91]

Anyone could see where this was going. Once again, instead of beleaguered Americans finally getting a hearing on illegal immigration, the media, along with their favorite Republicans, would bury them in one of their mock-a-thons. If you are opposed to illegal immigration, the elites in both parties would turn you into an object of ridicule.

Trump responded to McCain's belligerence toward his supporters by calling him a "dummy," leading to this exchange with Frank Luntz at the Family Leadership Summit, in Iowa.

> LUNTZ: Referring to John McCain, a war hero, five and a half years as a POW, and you call him a "dummy." Is that appropriate in running for president?
>
> TRUMP: You have to let me speak, Frank, because you interrupt all the time, okay? [*Laughter*] No, I know him too well, that's the problem.

Let's take John McCain. I'm in Phoenix. We have a meeting that is going to have five hundred people, at the Biltmore Hotel. We get a call from the hotel: It's turmoil. Thousands and thousands of people are showing up three, four days before—they're pitching tents on the hotel grass. The hotel says, *We can't handle this, it's gonna destroy the hotel.* We move it to the Convention Center. We have fifteen thousand people—the biggest one ever. Bigger than Bernie Sanders, bigger than—fifteen thousand people showed up to hear me speak. Bigger than anybody. And everybody knows it. A beautiful day with incredible people that were wonderful, great Americans, I will tell you.

John McCain goes, *Oh, boy, Trump makes my life difficult. He had fifteen thousand crazies show up.* "Crazies"—he called them all crazy. I said, *They weren't crazy. They were great Americans.* These people, if you would've seen these people—I know what a crazy is. I know all about crazies. These weren't crazy.

So he insulted me and he insulted everybody in that room. And I said, *Somebody should run against John McCain,* who has been, in my opinion, not so hot. And I supported him—I supported him for president. I raised a million dollars for him. That's a lot of money. I supported him. He lost, he let us down. But, you know, he lost. So I have never liked him as much after that, because I don't like losers. [*Laughter*]

But, Frank—Frank, let me get to it.

LUNTZ: He is a war hero, he's a war hero.

TRUMP: He hit me—he's not a war hero.

LUNTZ: Five and a half years in a Vietnamese prison camp.

TRUMP: He's a war hero because he was captured. I like people that weren't captured, okay? I hate to tell you. He was a war hero because he was captured, okay? And I believe—perhaps he is a war hero, but right now, he said some very bad things about a lot of people. So what I said is: *John McCain, I disagree with him, that these people aren't crazy.* And, very importantly, and I speak the truth, he graduated last in his class at Annapolis. So I said—nobody knows that—I said, *He graduated last, or second to last,* he graduated last in his class at Annapolis.[92]

Reading that, do you think the media gave you an accurate and honest account of what Trump said? He was justifiably angry at McCain for calling his supporters "crazies"—when Luntz interrupts him with the monumentally irrelevant "But he's a war hero!" Is that a pass for life? How long do we have to genuflect before this guy? Can we have a statute of limitations on how long a war hero gets to insult ordinary Americans? Maybe McCain reminds us of his valor a little too often.

Although Trump walked back the crack about McCain's heroism in his very next sentence, it left a mark. Despite sweeping condemnation of Trump, one week later, polls showed that veterans and those currently serving in the military preferred Trump to McCain, 53 percent to 41 percent. Trump's favorability among Republicans had nearly doubled, from 15 percent to 28 percent.[93] And those decent Americans humiliated by McCain at his 2008 town hall? I bet they didn't mind one bit when Trump said he preferred war heroes who weren't captured.

Fox News' Brit Hume had warned that the negative reaction to Trump's remark would be "widespread" and "quite damaging," because McCain "has a following in the party."[94]

But then it turned out McCain's only "following" was in the press corps. For the rest of the campaign, we didn't hear another peep out of the insufferable windbag *war hero.*

It's said that Trump is reckless, undisciplined, and shoots from the hip. If so, why does he always win these fights? A few times could be luck. When it's every time, we must consider the possibility that he's a much more brilliant strategist than anyone thought.

CHAPTER NINE

Disabled Reporter Joins
Media Effort to Create
More Disabled Americans

Apart from Trump's jab at John McCain, his most notorious attack was the one on former *Washington Post* reporter Serge Kovaleski, who is disabled. Believe nothing you've heard about that incident.

The truth is: after the 9/11 attack, the media were seized with affection for Muslims and decided that, henceforth, no unkind word could be uttered about Islam. They were worried sick that al-Qaeda might get its hands on a nuke and destroy an American city, because that might lead to discrimination against Muslims.

Trump came along and decided he wanted to protect America, so he didn't abide by the media's rules on discussing Muslims, making him public enemy number one. When Trump told a rally that thousands of Muslims in New Jersey had cheered the 9/11 attack, his statement was subjected to a forensic analysis that would never be applied to anything Hillary said.

The Washington Post's "Fact Checker" gave Trump "Four Pinocchios," so Trump produced a slew of contemporaneous news reports confirming that Muslims had cheered the 9/11 attack—the most hilarious of which was a story in the *Post* itself, by Serge Kovaleski. His article said, "In Jersey City, within hours of two jetliners' plowing into the World Trade Center, law enforcement authorities detained and questioned a number of people who were allegedly seen celebrating the attacks and holding tailgate-style parties on rooftops while they watched the devastation on the other side of the river."[95]

In response, Serge disavowed his own reporting. When Trump hit back, doing an imitation of Serge as a flailing imbecile for recanting his story, the media replied: *BUT HE'S DISABLED!*

Trump denied knowing that Serge was disabled, and demanded an apology, saying that anyone could see his imitation was of a flustered, frightened reporter, not a disabled person. It's true that Trump was not mimicking any mannerisms that Serge has. He doesn't jerk around or flail his arms. He's not retarded. He sits calmly, but if you look at his wrists, you'll see they are curved in. That's not the imitation Trump was doing—he was doing a standard retard, waving his arms and sounding stupid: "'Ahhh, I don't know what I said—ahhh, I don't remember!' He's going, 'Ahhh, I don't remember, maybe that's what I said!'"

The "disabled reporter" story wasn't about Serge, wasn't about the disabled, and was barely about Muslims. It was all about the media's PR campaign on behalf of Muslims. The media have been frantically pushing a Goebbels Big Lie about Islam ever since the World Trade Center came down. Their ability to destroy people had cowed the public into compliance with politically correct rules. But they couldn't intimidate Trump. So they made up a story about his making fun of a reporter's disability to distract from Kovaleski's article confirming Trump.

Everyone had seen Muslims celebrating around the world on 9/11, thrilled that thousands of innocent Americans had been slaughtered. New Yorkers saw some of that joy happening very close to home. (If it makes you happy, *New York Times*, students of Ward Churchill in Colorado saw it up close, too.)

The 2015 Paris attacks brought it all back. At Trump's rally right after that attack in November 2015—and a few weeks before the San Bernardino attack—he said, "Hey, I watched when the World Trade Center came tumbling down, and I watched in Jersey City, New Jersey, where thousands and thousands of people were cheering as that building was coming down. Thousands of people were *cheering*."

Trump was speaking as an enraged New Yorker, talking the way normal people talk. He was not giving testimony under oath. He was not writing *The 9/11 Commission Report*. No one takes it literally when someone says, "I called you a thousand times," or, "There were a million people in there." It wasn't that Americans didn't care whether there were "hundreds" or "thousands" of Muslims celebrating in Jersey City. They knew Trump was telling the truth, and the truth is: after three thousand innocent Americans were murdered there were widespread celebrations by Muslims.

Committed to the idea that the real victims of 9/11 were Muslims, the media reacted as if Trump had called Obama the N-word. The one point they had been VERY clear on after 9/11 was that Muslims were not to blame for the attack and Americans should redouble their efforts to be nice to them.

The media's original charge against Trump was not just that he was exaggerating by saying that "thousands" of Muslims had celebrated the attack, but that, in fact, absolutely *no* Muslims had cheered the attack. The media's position was: *If there were no news stories about something we were determined not to report, it didn't happen.*

In fact, however, there was plenty of evidence that lots of Muslims in New Jersey had celebrated 9/11.

- On September 16, 2001, WCBS-TV's Pablo Guzmán reported that the FBI had raided a building in Jersey City "swarming with suspects" who had been seen celebrating after seeing the planes slam into the World Trade Center.[96]

- A September 22, 2001, *San Francisco Chronicle* article reported that police in Jersey City had "detained several men seen 'celebrating' the attack as the smoke first rose across the river."[97]

- An MTV video called "Fight for Your Rights: Aftermath of Terror" that aired on November 17, 2001, featured a high school senior, Emily Acevedo, telling MTV that she had seen Muslims celebrating the 9/11 attacks outside the Paterson, New Jersey, town hall. On camera, she said she saw "a lot of people . . . chanting and raving," "holding rocks and sticks," and "saying, 'Burn America.'"[98]

- The day after 9/11, four people called into *The Howard Stern Show* with eyewitness accounts of Muslims celebrating in Paterson. (Yes, it was Howard Stern, but this was the day after the attack. It was a somber broadcast.)[99]

- A September 14, 2001, *New York Post* op-ed included this line: "Here in New York, it was easy to get angry listening to Egyptians, Palestinians and the Arabs of nearby Paterson, N.J., celebrate as they received word of the murderous attacks in New York and Washington."[100]

- Even *The New York Times* had a human interest story on September 30, 2001, reporting "rumors" of "Muslim celebrations in the wake of the trade center attacks."[101] Apparently no one at the *Times* found that worthy of investigation. Would that the *Times* had a news-gathering arm!

- And then there was the article by the disabled guy, Serge Kovaleski, in *The Washington Post* on September 18, 2001, reporting that police had questioned a number of people in Jersey City seen "celebrating."[102]

The only reason there weren't even more "news clips" of Muslims celebrating 9/11 was that the moment the planes slammed into the World Trade Center, the media turned themselves into defense lawyers for Islam. It was their method of grieving. The day after the 9/11 attack, with live human beings still trapped under the rubble, a *New York Times* editorial expressed concern that "Americans of Islamic descent" would become "the target for another period of American xenophobia and ethnic discrimination."[103]

Soon the *Times* was brimming with stories of terrified Muslims cowering in fear of Americans, in articles with titles like these: "Attacks and Harassment of Arab-Americans Increase," "Arabs and Muslims Steer Through an Unsettling Scrutiny," and "For Arab-Americans, Flag-Flying and Fear." There were Muslim women afraid to leave their homes in Islamic attire, veiled death threats left on answering machines at the United Nations, a man allegedly holding a sign in a Muslim area of Brooklyn that said, *Get out of our country,* vandalism of one Arab store in Virginia and one mosque in California, and a Muslim who had "heard sporadic reports of harassment."[104]

In other news, America had just suffered the most deadly terrorist attack in recorded history.

So, no, we didn't expect Muslims celebrating the 9/11 attack to receive the lavish coverage accorded college rape hoaxes. The fact that *The New York Times* didn't report something is not proof that it didn't happen. Newspapers in the Reconstruction South probably didn't have a lot of stories about Klan violence.

After Trump's remark at the rally about Muslims celebrating in Jersey City, ABC's George Stephanopoulos informed Trump that the police chief of Jersey City said there were no Muslims celebrating 9/11:

> STEPHANOPOULOS: You know, the police say that didn't happen, and all those rumors have been on the Internet for some time. So did you misspeak yesterday?

TRUMP: It did happen. I saw it. It was on television; I saw it.

STEPHANOPOULOS: You saw that with your own eyes? Police say it didn't happen.

TRUMP: George, it did happen. There were people that were cheering on the other side of New Jersey, where you have large Arab populations. They were cheering as the World Trade Center came down. I know it might be not politically correct for you to talk about it, but there were people cheering as that building came down—as those buildings came down. And that tells you something. It was well covered at the time, George. Now, I know they don't like to talk about it, but it was well covered at the time. There were people over in New Jersey that were watching it, a heavy Arab population, that were cheering as the buildings came down. *Not good.*

STEPHANOPOULOS: As I said, the police have said it didn't happen.

The Washington Post's "Fact Checker," Glenn Kessler, was bowled over by the fact that Trump refused to back down even after Stephanopoulos had confronted him with "Police say it didn't happen." The media had put no small effort into intimidating government officials into giving the official line on Muslims, and now Trump was refusing to accept their lies! How could the press begin to deal with someone who had not been silenced by "Police say it didn't happen"?

Can we get that on the record? When a police chief says something, we all go home, no more questions, it's over? Because if that's the rule, it has to be applied in all cases—not just when the media are defending Muslims but also in cases of police brutality, civilian shootings, Ferguson, Baltimore, Eric Garner—the whole nine yards.

Turning to his own fact-checking duties, Kessler said that

proving Muslims hadn't celebrated 9/11 was "like writing about the hole in the doughnut—how can you write about nothing?" But his team at the *Post* went to work and found . . . nothing. Kessler reported that an "extensive examination of news clips from that period turns up nothing." There were no celebrations by Arabs anywhere in New Jersey. Despite their intensive review of news archives, the fact-checkers somehow missed Serge Kovaleski's article in their own newspaper.

For the final coup de grâce, Kessler quoted Jersey City's Democratic mayor, Steven Fulop—"who is a possible Democratic candidate for governor in 2017"—affirming that "no one in Jersey City cheered on Sept. 11." Of course, untrusting people who aren't convinced by "Police say it didn't happen" probably aren't going to accept the word of a Democratic politician running for office in a state with a large Muslim population, either.

More confirmation for Trump came in after his statement at the rally:

- On CNN, former mayor Rudy Giuliani corroborated Trump, saying, "The police department set up a unit, and we kept track of it for about three or four weeks. And we had some attacks. And we did have some celebrating. That is true. We had pockets of celebration, some in Queens, some in Brooklyn."[105]

    NJ Advance Media talked to retired Jersey City police captain Peter Gallagher, who said that he personally had "cleared a rooftop celebration of 20 to 30 people" at 6 Tonnele Avenue, in Jersey City, soon after the second tower fell. On the rooftop, he said, "some men were dancing, some held kids on their shoulders," and "women were shouting in Arabic and keening in the high-pitched wail of Arabic fashion." He told them to go back into their apartments for their own safety.[106]

- Retired officer Arthur Teeter, who was working in the radio room at Jersey City police headquarters on September 11, said he had gotten so many calls about Muslim rooftop celebrations, "it was disturbing—that's the only word I can use."[107]
- At least two civilian witnesses, Ron Knight and Carlos Ferran, reported seeing Arabs celebrating and shouting, *"Allahu Akbar!"* on John F. Kennedy Boulevard in Jersey City. "They were happy," Ferran said. They had "their hands in the air."[108]
- Eleven Jersey City police officers claimed on Facebook to have been witnesses to Arab celebrations.[109]

    Three officers who still worked for the Jersey City police, including a "high-ranking official," also confirmed the celebrations but were unable to speak for attribution, *for fear they would "run afoul of Jersey City Mayor Steven Fulop, who has repeatedly said celebrations did not take place."*[110] (Emphasis added.)

Yes, that would be the same Mayor Fulop who George Stephanopoulos and Glenn Kessler cited as proof that Trump was wrong—a guy who was putting political pressure on the police to lie and say there were no Muslims celebrating on 9/11.

That adds up to more than two dozen people reporting separate and distinct instances of between a dozen and forty Muslims celebrating the 9/11 attacks in the New York vicinity, at a minimum of six different locations—two street addresses in Jersey City, at least two in Paterson, and somewhere in Queens and Brooklyn, as Mayor Giuliani's police reports stated. And this was in the face of a media and political culture determined to suppress negative information about Muslims.

At that point, the media's big argument with Trump came down to his saying "thousands" and not "hundreds." FOUR PINOC-CHIOS!

Suddenly the media became very punctilious about the facts. MTV admitted that, yes, its documentary did show Emily Acevedo saying on camera that she'd seen Arabs celebrating the 9/11 attacks in front of the Paterson town hall, but—ha!—she'd only said it was "a lot of people," *not* "thousands." This riposte was in an article titled "Trump Is Wrong About People 'Cheering' 9/11 in New Jersey—We Dug Up the Video That Proves It."[111]

Tommy Christopher at *Mediaite* complained that "Giuliani doesn't say how these 'facts' were corroborated." According to Christopher, unless the Muslims specifically told the cops, "Well, we were kinda celebrating," the NYPD's alleged "corroboration" meant nothing.[112] (On the other hand, the fact that the politically ambitious mayor of Jersey City *denied* there were celebrations without any investigation whatsoever constituted airtight proof.)

As for the *New York Post* writer who said he'd listened "to Egyptians, Palestinians and the Arabs of nearby Paterson, N.J., celebrate as they received word of the murderous attacks in New York and Washington," PolitiFact retorted, "This article contains no official documentation or evidence to corroborate the claim, so it is not proof."[113] (The prevalence of cell phone videos and surveillance cameras since 2001 has been a disaster for the left. If we hadn't seen the surveillance footage of "Big Mike" Brown knocking over a cigar store in Ferguson, Missouri, the media would still be telling us about "gentle giant" Mike Brown.)

The Washington Post's Kessler dismissed the numerous eyewitness accounts of Muslims celebrating as "anecdotal." Instead, he had reliable sources like a Muslim professor, politically correct politicians, and an unnamed "man who said he walked up and down through Jersey City on 9/11"—all saying they didn't see any Muslims celebrating.

The article by Serge Kovaleski in his own newspaper was trickier for Kessler to discount. For this one, Kessler prissily announced that "a number of people" does not equal "thousands." So Trump still got his four Pinocchios. Kessler also complained that there was "no video footage or other proof."[114]

After ruling all proof inadmissible, the media announced that there was no "proof" for Trump's claim.

It would be great if journalists were this exacting about other stories they foist on the public—for example, their potboilers about police brutality, global warming, white supremacists, and fraternity rapes. What is the proof that there is any police brutality? Did any police officer ever admit, "Well, we were kinda beating up innocent civilians"? If not, then Tommy Christopher is not buying it. And if you say there are "thousands" of cases of police brutality when you mean "a lot," MTV rules the story: WRONG ABOUT POLICE VIOLENCE.

The media were appalled that Trump remembered "thousands" of Muslims celebrating 9/11—when the number was (probably) "more than a hundred"—but didn't mind when President Bill Clinton claimed to remember "black churches being burned in my own state when I was a child"—when that number was *zero*. Despite Clinton's "vivid and painful memories" of these apocryphal black church burnings, Little Rock's *Arkansas Democrat-Gazette* checked with: the state historian, the current and past president of the Arkansas NAACP, the former president of the Regular Arkansas Baptist Convention, and the chairman of the Arkansas Black History Advisory Committee, all of who confirmed there were no black church burnings in Arkansas in that period.[115]

The media were shocked when Trump said "Jersey City" rather than "New Jersey and the outer boroughs"—but didn't make a peep when Clinton invented an apocryphal increase in black church burnings and blamed it on "racial hostility."

To the contrary, the media joined Clinton's hoax campaign against nonexistent white supremacists burning black churches with major articles on the fake epidemic in newspapers all across the country, including *The New York Times, The Washington Post,* and *The Boston Globe,* not to mention a major three-part series in *USA Today.*

It fell to investigative reporter Michael Fumento—not *The Washington Post* fact-checker—to actually check facts and establish that there had been no increase in black church burnings in the previous decade. They had been decreasing—right up until the president and the media invented the church-burning hoax, and inspired copycats.[116]

Clinton's lies weren't inconsequential pop-offs at a rally. His church-burning tall tale led to the creation of a multi-agency task force with two hundred FBI and ATF agents and a multimillion-dollar spending bill to stop "the fires of hatred and bigotry."

A few months later, Clinton became the first president in history to knowingly make a false statement while giving the keynote address at a major party convention. He did so merely to accuse white soldiers of racism, whereas Trump's mistatement made the sickening suggestion that Muslims are not 100 percent, law-abiding, and America-loving.

At the 1996 Democratic National Convention, Clinton said black soldiers had recently found swastikas painted on their doors at Fort Bragg.[117] "We still have too many Americans," Clinton sadly explained, "who give in to their fears of those who are different from them." When he said that, he already knew that the prime suspect was the black "victim" himself. A few months later, the soldier was discharged for concocting this fake hate crime.[118]

And as long as we're suddenly so finicky about every little word, Clinton had also lied when he said the black soldiers were members of Special Forces. They were not. FOUR PINOCCHIOS!

It would almost be worth giving in to the media's inane "fact-checking" of Trump if we could have this new standard of proof applied to all news.

Kessler isn't a fact-checker; he's running a Democratic Party hit operation. Other news outlets quote "The Fact Checker" as if it's an objective report, like a DNA test. No, Kessler is offended by everything Republicans say.

Even within a media culture this shameless, Serge Kovaleski's denial of his own contemporaneous news story was remarkable. One week after 9/11, Serge reported that Muslims in Jersey City had been seen "celebrating the attacks and holding tailgate-style parties." Apparently, in the stress and emotion after 9/11, he had made the mistake of reporting something true without realizing he was violating liberal orthodoxy. Since then, of course, the media have made clear that, for launching a devastating attack on America, Muslims have become the moral equivalent of civil rights marchers.

So when Trump cited that story, Serge denied it, telling CNN's Brian Stelter, "That was not the case, as best I can remember.'"[119]

In order to say Trump was wrong, reporters were willing to call themselves liars. This was the Goebbels-style propaganda about Islam that Trump was up against. Trump was the only politician man enough to say things that were obviously true. And when the entire media-political establishment reacted like scalded cats, he punched back twice as hard.

The media screamed that Serge was "disabled" only to prevent Trump from mentioning that *Washington Post* story ever again. Since when do the media care about the disabled? I don't remember a lot of gnashing of teeth when Fox's *Family Guy* made fun of Sarah Palin's Down syndrome child, Trig.

They didn't want the public to notice that what Trump had said about Muslims celebrating was fundamentally true and what the media told us about Muslims was fundamentally false. Americans knew perfectly well that after the 9/11 attack, we didn't see Arabs in capitals around the world sobbing hysterically. We saw celebrations, including in our own country. The left thought that with enough intimidation, they could convince us of anything, as if the underlying truth didn't matter. But they hadn't counted on Trump.

CHAPTER TEN

Islam's PR Agency: The American Media

One thing the guys who planned 9/11 never expected was that Muslims would become a protected class in America. They must have thought, *Boy, are we going to be hated!* Instead, since that attack, we've admitted another two million Muslim immigrants, we almost built a mosque at Ground Zero, colleges are teaching classes on "Islamophobia" (defined as: "believing what they clearly say"), and the U.S. State Department tells Muslim countries, *We are pleased to present you with this giant check for one hundred mosques.*[120] Why, thank you!

Importing millions of immigrants whose religion teaches them that we are Satan—when we don't have to take any—is the new Selma. We were supposed to accept that Islamic terrorism—something that never existed in this country before Teddy Kennedy's 1965 immigration act—was just a part of life, a wonderful slice of the vibrant fabric of America. If you disagreed, you were a racist.

The first step after any terrorist attack was for government officials and the media to deny that it had been committed by Muslims, and even if it was, it had nothing to do with Islam. Once that position became inoperative, they would figure out some way to blame the attack on Americans—for not being diverse enough, tolerant enough, or supportive enough of amnesty.

After the slaughter of soldiers at Fort Hood in 2009 by a Muslim army major yelling, *"Allahu Akbar!"* President Obama warned Americans not to "jump to conclusions"—namely, the obvious conclusion that the attack was an act of Islamic terrorism. As conclusions go, it wasn't much of a jump. Army chief of staff General George Casey went on *Meet the Press* and said, "As horrific as this tragedy was, if our diversity becomes a casualty, I think that's worse." Evelyn Waugh couldn't have written it better.

On May 3, 2010, a truck bomb was found smoldering in Times Square. That night, Mayor Michael Bloomberg went on *CBS Evening News* and said he suspected it was "somebody homegrown," maybe "somebody with a political agenda that doesn't like the health care bill or something."[121] Police released a photo of a suspect, "described as a white male in his forties."[122] For twenty-four hours, everybody was looking for a balding white guy who was angry about Obamacare. Then it turned out to be another Muslim—who our government, in its amazingly rigorous vetting process, had made a citizen one year earlier.

When howling, savage Muslims besieged the American consulate in Benghazi, Libya, on 9/11/2012, murdering our ambassador and three other Americans, the Obama administration blamed an amateur American filmmaker who'd made a video critical of the Prophet Muhammad, peace be upon him. At the funeral for Tyrone Woods, one of the two retired Navy SEALs killed in Benghazi, Secretary of State Hillary Clinton told his father, "We're going to have that person arrested and prosecuted that did the video." This was despite knowing full well that it "had nothing to do" with the movie—as Hillary told the president of Egypt, as well as her daughter, Chelsea, the day after the attack.[123]

After Muslim immigrants bombed the 2013 Boston Marathon, former CIA director Michael Hayden went on *Fox News Sunday with Chris Wallace* and said, "Immigration to this country contributes to our national security," adding, "We welcome these kinds of folks coming to the United States."[124] It was as if he had just woken up and didn't know what had happened. Representative Paul Ryan, Conscience of a Nation, demanded that Congress pass an amnesty bill, saying, "If anything, what we see in Boston is that we have to fix and modernize our immigration system."

The day after two Pakistani Muslim first- and second-generation immigrants shot up the San Bernardino community center, killing fourteen people, the attorney general of the United States, Loretta Lynch, said that her "greatest fear" was the "disturbing rise of anti-Muslim rhetoric."[125]

The morning after the 2016 terrorist attack on the gay nightclub in Orlando, Jim Cavanaugh, a former official at the Bureau of Alcohol, Tobacco, Firearms and Explosives and an NBC News law enforcement analyst, said that his best guess was that the shooter might have been "rooted in white hate movements," and had picked the club "because it's a diverse club and he hates diverse people."[126]

Twenty years ago, terrorism expert Steven Emerson ruined his career by going on TV the night of the Oklahoma City bombing and saying the attack had all the earmarks of Islamic terrorism.[127] Emerson has been reviled for that statement ever since—his name cannot be mentioned without it coming up. It will be in his obituary. But today, we're required to falsely blame Americans for every Islamic jihadist's attack.

HIDE THE MUSLIM, WIN A PULITZER

Initial reports about the San Bernardino mass shooting on December 2, 2015, said there were one to three shooters, heavily armed, possibly wearing body armor, who had burst into a party at the community center, started shooting, reloaded, and shot again, leaving at least twenty people dead or injured.

Even making allowances for the fog of war in breaking news, it sure sounded like an act of terrorism. Soon, the name of one of the suspected shooters from a police scanner was circulating in the news: "Farook Syed" (as it was first reported).

The media took an eternity just to nail down how many shooters there were. *One* vs. *more than one* was a crucial fact. Public massacres are committed by either the mentally ill or Muslims, and psychotics almost never work in teams. The last time a mass slaughter was committed by as many as two non-Muslims was nearly twenty years ago, in Columbine, Colorado.

So it was significant when a police shootout with the killers a few hours later established that there were at least two shooters and they both happened to be Muslim—which we found out from the persistent warnings not to discriminate against Muslims. On MSNBC, for example, former police officer Eugene O'Donnell said that law enforcement nationwide would be on red alert to "make sure there's not copycat incidents *against Muslims*."[128]

Today, the San Bernardino attack joins a list of about a dozen Islamic terrorist attacks in the U.S. since 9/11. But the night of the attack, TV commentators were mostly reminded of Adam Lanza and Dylann Roof—lone white male psychopaths. ABC, NBC, CNN, MSNBC, and Fox News all compared San Bernardino to these mass shootings by white men who should have been in straitjackets, which bear no relationship to mass murders committed by a team, such as 9/11, the Boston Marathon, the London subway bombing, *Charlie Hebdo,* and the recent Paris attack. According to Nexis, the only people to mention Paris and Fort Hood were Aaron Cohen and Jim Hanson on Fox News.

In addition to avoiding reporting that the attack was committed by two people—as well as the indelicate fact that they were Muslims—the media threw everyone off the scent with a report from *The Los*

Angeles Times claiming that one of the perpetrators had gotten into an argument with someone at the community center and stormed back twenty minutes later, guns blazing. This was an incredibly important detail to be dropped into the news cycle, because it clearly pointed to workplace violence. Except, apparently, it wasn't true—which the *Times* discreetly admitted a month later.[129]

It was just invented by some anonymous law enforcement official, passed on to the newspaper, and injected into breaking news coverage. This prevented virtually every analyst on TV from suggesting the attack was terrorism for at least another twenty-four hours.

That night, for example, MSNBC's Chris Hayes repeatedly said that *The L.A. Times*—"an excellent news organization"—was reporting that "a dispute at a holiday gathering may have sparked the mass shooting. . . . There was actually some kind of argument; someone left and came back." NBC News correspondent Tom Costello confirmed, "It is highly unlikely that this was any sort of jihadi type of terrorism." NBC News justice correspondent Pete Williams said, "The working assumption is that this was, in fact, some sort of workplace violence shooting."[130]

The false report of a workplace dispute was never revisited, never explained, never justified, never explicitly retracted. It just quietly disappeared from the story. Knowing that it had been lied to, why didn't *The L.A. Times* ever name names? A government official intentionally provided false information to the public about a terrorist attack, well after both terrorists were dead. If there was a law enforcement purpose, what was it? If there was none—and this was just another Muslim cover-up—isn't a free press supposed to expose corruption?

Suppose the cops had lied to the press about James Holmes's mass murder at an Aurora, Colorado, movie theater, putting out a bogus story that Holmes was a Muslim? Do you think we would know that officer's name? Yes, I think we would!

But when it comes to Muslim terrorism, it's Pulitzer-worthy

reporting to jam up the news cycle with false flag information about "workplace violence." *The L.A. Times* won a Pulitzer for its San Bernardino coverage.[131]

IGNORE INCONVENIENT FACTS, OBSESS OVER "BORN IN AMERICA"

Muslim terrorists in America are invariably billed as "home-grown," or—now that we're dealing with the children of immigrants let in under Teddy Kennedy's immigration act—"American." The media would tell us only the nation listed on the terrorists' passports and then act indignant if anyone suggested there was any difference between a tenth-generation American and an Afghan whose parents had immigrated here in the 1980s.

Luckily, one of the San Bernardino terrorists was born in the United States, so we had nonstop references to Syed Farook as "American"—probably of the Back Bay Farooks. This second-generation Pakistani immigrant had committed the mass murder with his very recently immigrated Pakistani wife, Tashfeen Malik. According to *The New York Times,* that made them: "homegrown."

The Denver Post called Farook "an American citizen, born in Chicago." Headlines in the *Chicago Tribune* referred to the Pakistani jihadist wife, just off the boat, as a "'Modern' Girl, 'Traditional' Wife," and a "Calif. Killer." *The Washington Post* reported that police had identified Syed as "a county health worker born in Chicago." The *Los Angeles Times* noted that Farook had been "born in Chicago and raised in Riverside."

Why a "California couple" would stockpile guns and bombs to kill Americans remained a total mystery.

The day after the attack, President Obama said, "It is possible that this is terrorist-related, but we don't know. It is also possible that this was workplace-related."[132] *The Washington Post* ran the headline "Terrorism? Workplace Violence? The Search for a Motive in San Bernardino." Having had twenty-four hours to process the scene, David Bowdich, assistant director of the FBI's Los Angeles field office, said, "It would be irresponsible and premature for me to call this terrorism."[133] (I think we may be zeroing in on *The L.A. Times'* "law enforcement source.")

Whenever a white cop shoots a black kid, the race and ethnicity of everyone involved is monumentally relevant. But when it came to terrorism, it was rude to mention ethnicity.

After a dozen Middle Eastern men killed 130 people in simultaneous attacks in Paris, on November 13, 2015, *The New York Times* insisted on calling the terrorists "French" and "Belgian."[134] Readers would be left with the impression that the attack was committed by guys who looked like Gérard Depardieu. A *Times* editorial triumphantly proclaimed that "the first gunman to be conclusively identified, Omar Ismail Mostefai, was not a refugee, but a French citizen born and raised in a town just south of Paris."[135]

Ismail is "French" in the same way that Caitlin Jenner is a "woman."

That doesn't mean we can draw no conclusions about the relative strength of men and women, even though a "woman" won the decathlon at the 1976 Olympics.

Anyone could see the Paris terrorists were unassimilated Middle Easterners. True, they'd learned French because otherwise they'd have a problem with the welfare office and might not be able to get their checks. The media feigned confusion. *What do you mean Middle Eastern? It says right here on his passport that he's a Belgian national. Stop peeking at the photos!*

It was a two-step process to keep exonerating Muslims for their repeated terrorist attacks:

1. Use some ridiculous classification system in order to mislabel Middle Eastern Muslims as "French" or "American" on a technicality;
2. Seize on that misclassification as the centerpiece of your argument.

It was as if the *Times* had gotten "rhinoceros" accidentally classified as a "sheep," and then proceeded to write a whole scientific paper claiming there are scaly-skinned, two-horned sheep in Africa. Anyone would look at the picture and say: *That's a rhinoceros!* Similarly, people looked at photos of the "French" and "Belgian" citizens who attacked Paris and said, *Those are Middle Easterners!*

At some point, people were going to trust their lying eyes. If the *Times* would prefer, we'll call them "French-born Middle Eastern terrorists," but if they don't accept that, in another thirty seconds, we're going back to "Middle Eastern terrorists."

I ALMOST FEEL SORRY FOR THE JIHADISTS

It must have been frustrating for Muslim jihadists to have politicians and journalists constantly refusing to acknowledge their terrorism. No matter how clearly the terrorists indicated they were killing infidels for ISIS or al-Qaeda or Allah, American elites resolutely refused to believe them.

Both the San Bernardino and Orlando terrorists pledged allegiance to ISIS *while committing their attacks*.

These were some of the headlines after San Bernardino:

"Motive for Calif. Killings a Mystery"—*Chicago Tribune*, December 4, 2015

"Motive for Attack Unknown"—*The Denver Post*, December 4, 2015

"A Couple's Inexplicable Path"—*Los Angeles Times*, December 5, 2015

"San Bernardino Shooting: Was It Workplace Violence or Terrorism?"—NPR's *Morning Edition*, December 3, 2015

Two Muslims chattering with one another for a year about jihad and martyrdom commit a mass murder while pledging their allegiance to ISIS—and the media refused to believe them.

The Orlando terrorist, Omar Mateen, had told co-workers he had ties to Islamic terrorist groups. He took at least two trips to Saudi Arabia. Acting on tips from concerned citizens, the FBI investigated Mateen for terrorism twice. In the middle of committing the most deadly mass shooting in U.S. history, Mateen took the trouble to call both 911 and a local news station to say he was doing it for ISIS and to praise his "homeboys," the Boston Marathon bombers.

Media: *Does anyone know if was he a member of the NRA? Did he struggle with his sexuality because of our homophobic American culture?*

Here are some headlines in *The Washington Post* after Mateen's slaughter:

"The Target Was a Gay Nightclub. The Target Was Also All of Us; The Latest Anti-Gay Attack Comes at a High Point of LGBT Acceptance"

"Orlando Shooting: The Key Things to Know About Guns and Mass Shootings in America"

"Before Orlando: A Look at Crimes Against the Gay Community"

"The Orlando Shooting Shows Again That It Always Comes Back to the Guns"

"There Was Another Terrible Case of Gun Violence over the
    Weekend"
"A Horrible Day for Orlando, Gay Pride and U.S. History"

While at Walter Reed Medical Center, Major Nidal Malik
Hasan gave what was supposed to be a medical lecture on how
non-Muslims should be decapitated, set on fire, and have burning
oil poured down their throats.[136] He was in close contact with the
radical imam Anwar al-Awlaki. He shouted, *"Allahu Akbar!"* before
gunning down soldiers at Fort Hood.

The media responded to Hasan's attack with lachrymose accounts of the "Islamophobia" he had suffered at the hands of Americans. An ALLAH IS LOVE bumper sticker was torn off his car! NPR
interviewed a former Muslim army chaplain who said that he
"never met a Muslim service member who didn't at some time or
other face some sort of harassment or being made fun of for being
a Muslim American."[137]

The New York Times ran one editorial and two op-eds the day
after the attack, explaining that Hasan committed the attack because he was stressed, followed by news stories like, "Painful Stories Take a Toll on Military Therapists" and "When Soldiers'
Minds Snap."

After Obama labeled the Fort Hood attack an act of "workplace violence," Hasan's spiritual adviser denounced his administration for a lack of transparency in refusing to admit that it was
terrorism. When Omar Mateen's ISIS-inspired attack led the media to denounce it as an act of "homophobia," the al-Qaeda magazine, *Inspire*, ordered jihadists in America to stop killing minorities
and concentrate on Anglo-Saxons, to avoid sending a confusing
message.[138]

What do Muslims have to do to have their terrorism taken
seriously?

• • •

It took the media all of six seconds to smoke out the motive for Dylann Roof's massacre. There was no confusion about the motive in that case. It was racism—deep, immutable racism. And all Americans were guilty. (At least we could finally have that national conversation about race we've all been looking forward to.) Karen Attiah wrote in *The Washington Post* that the attack served as a "reminder that racism and white supremacy continue to course through America's veins."[139] An op-ed in *The New York Times* complained about the "rush to dissociate other white Americans from his violence."[140]

The Charleston shooting was the first white-on-black mass murder in America in at least a century, going back to the Klan days. How many Americans have to be slaughtered by Muslims in the first two decades of the twenty-first century before—to paraphrase *The New York Times'* op-ed page—we stop dissociating other Muslims from Muslim violence?

Media: *That's the wrong lesson!*

The main lesson we were supposed to take from 9/11 was: *Don't be mean to Muslims!* The main lesson from Fort Hood was: *It was some American's fault for scraping a bumper sticker off Nidal Hasan's car.* The main lesson from the murderous attack on our embassy in Benghazi was: *It was an American moviemaker's fault.* The main lesson from the Times Square bombing was: *We think it was a white guy.* The main lesson of the Boston Marathon was: *It's our fault for not passing an amnesty bill!* The main lesson from San Bernardino was: *Our greatest fear is that Americans will engage in violence against Muslims.* The main lesson from the Orlando nightclub slaughter was: *It's America's homophobic culture!*

There ought to be a game show with journalists called *Blame the American*!

QUESTION: Okay, an epidemic of dengue fever breaks out in Singapore. How do you blame Americans?

NEW YORK TIMES REPORTER: [*BUZZ!*] Asians are taught to hate themselves because of white American models, so they develop low self-esteem, leading them to not take proper care of themselves . . .

QUESTION: The Taliban plays soccer with decapitated human heads. How is that America's fault?

TIM KING, SALEM-NEWS.COM: [*BUZZ!*] It's America's fault for not stepping in after the Soviets left and establishing a legitimate government and health care facilities! (King actually wrote that article.)[141]

Democrats and Republicans may have disagreed about some things, but they spoke as one in always blaming Americans first and holding Muslims harmless. It was working beautifully, too— until Trump wrecked everything!

The single overriding principle in our society is that Americans are the worst, and every other ethnicity, religion, or nationality is horribly oppressed by us. Hillary Clinton, Speaker Paul Ryan, Barack Obama, Governor Nikki Haley, and the anonymous law enforcement official inventing a workplace violence incident for the San Bernardino shooters all agree. Republican Senator Bob Bennett agrees! (Agreed—until he went to his death apologizing to Muslims for Donald Trump.) We're the worst people on earth and the sooner we can replace ourselves, the better.

And then Donald Trump appeared. After a decade of terrorist attacks that were the direct result of U.S. immigration policy, and the only consequence was more Muslim immigration, he had a new idea. He thought that Americans shouldn't have to die so that no Muslim's feelings get hurt.

CHAPTER ELEVEN

Now We Know Why They Don't Want to Talk about Muslim Immigration

A week after the San Bernardino attack—which followed the Paris attack, the Oklahoma beheading attack, the Chattanooga military center attack, the Times Square attack, the Boston Marathon attack, the Fort Hood attack, the diaper bomber attack, the shoe bomb attack, the Washington, D.C., sniper attack, and the 9/11 attack—Trump suggested we take a pause in Muslim immigration.

The condescending class's position was: *No, you can't address that issue.* It was tacky to talk about ending the government's policy of bringing in immigrants who want to kill us.

A run of rape hoaxes at Duke, Columbia, and Virginia universities is a valid reason to discuss "campus rape culture." A Muslim teen bringing a clock designed to look like a bomb to school, and then being briefly detained after refusing to cooperate with police, is a valid reason to discuss "Islamophobia." A female presidential candidate whose speeches make children cry and dogs run from the room was a reason to discuss the sexism inherent in calling women's voices "shrill."

But first- and second-generation Muslim immigrants slaughtering 130 people in Paris and then, two weeks later, gunning down fourteen Americans in San Bernardino was NOT sufficient reason to discuss Muslim immigration.

The Washington Post's Philip Bump indignantly replied to Trump's proposal, saying, "There is, in fact, no reliable evidence that a large percentage of Muslims in the United States—or, for that matter, Muslims hoping to travel to the United States—support doing harm to the country or plan to commit acts of violence."

There's evidence that *some* of them do. Why do we need to take that risk?

While it's great news that most Muslim immigrants aren't terrorists—and thank you very much for that contribution, Philip—as Samuel Johnson said, "a horse that can count to ten is a remarkable horse, not a remarkable mathematician." We want remarkable immigrants, not immigrants whose main selling point is "hasn't gunned down fifty people in a gay nightclub yet."

Anyone with a brain cell could see that admitting Muslim refugees increased the odds of a terrorist attack in a way that admitting white Western Europeans would not.

What's the upside of admitting 100,000 poor, culturally backward, non-English-speaking Muslims every year? The government fraud? The clitorectomies? Overburdening our schools and hospitals? The honor killings? Muslim "refugees" are far more likely to be on welfare than our own native-born. Can't we at least discriminate against people who plan to access government programs that are supposed to tide over our own citizens when they fall on hard times?

The American taxpayer is also saddled with the additional cost of "vetting" Muslim immigrants, as well as the cost of surveilling them once they're here. There are currently more than a thousand active investigations of ISIS in all fifty states, requiring ever-expanding law enforcement agencies to track, wiretap, and investigate immigrants with possible terrorist sympathies.

It's like being offered a dumpster full of crushed rock, 99 percent of which is ordinary gravel—but 1 percent is a very toxic poison. *Have at it, gentlemen!* It would be one thing if the dumpster were 1 percent solid gold nuggets. But with Muslim immigration, on one hand there's a downside, but on the other hand there's a HUGE downside. It took only one Muslim in Orlando, two Muslims in San Bernardino, eight Muslims in Paris, two at the Boston Marathon, one at a Chattanooga military recruitment center, one at Fort Hood, and nineteen on 9/11 to cause mass devastation. It doesn't take many, and we don't need any.

The "advantages" of Muslim immigration are all utterly bogus. NPR listeners would cite "diversity," but that's a benefit that exists entirely in the heads of liberals, experienced only when they go to a themed restaurant.

With other problems, we make the best of something we can't change. Immigration is the definition of something we can change. Billions of people don't live in America. We can admit them or not admit them for any reason we choose. We could say: only redheads, only people over six feet tall, only people born in December, or—Trump's suggestion—only people whose religion does not instruct them that we are infidels who deserve to die.

Neither Republican nor Democratic administrations mind inconveniencing American citizens at airports because of terrorism. Why is it such an intolerable inconvenience to make certain foreigners, who have no right to come to this country, ever, wait a few years, until, as Trump says, we can figure out what the hell is going on?

This was not a discussion the media wanted to have. Republicans, Democrats, liberal and conservative pundits, foreign and domestic commentators—all rose in unison to denounce Trump. Then he did something completely unprecedented: He didn't back down. Spoiled by decades of Republicans asking *Who do I apologize to?*, the elites were not prepared for someone who doesn't care what they think.

AMERICA'S GOTTA GO—THAT'S NOT WHO WE ARE

Forced to formulate arguments against Trump's proposed moratorium on Muslim immigration, it became clear why politicians and journalists never wanted to have this discussion in the first place. Their main argument against a temporary Muslim ban was to gasp in horror and call Trump names. Their backup arguments were straw men, nitpicking, and lies.

BuzzFeed editor Ben Smith responded to Trump's proposed Muslim ban by sending out a memo informing his writers that they now were allowed to call Trump a "racist": "It is, for instance, entirely fair to call [Trump] a mendacious racist . . . He's out there saying things that are false, and running an overtly anti-Muslim campaign. BuzzFeed News' reporting is rooted in facts, not opinion; these are facts."

BuzzFeed's little announcement illustrates the axiom that anything liberals don't have an answer for will be called racist. There's nothing racist about a Muslim ban. A religion is a set a beliefs, not a genetic code in your DNA. You can be born to Muslim parents, but you can't be born believing something.

We're at war, and the enemy is justifying its slaughter of innocent men, women, and children as a tenet of its religion. We're not talking about people who are "Muslim" in the sense that they eat pita and lamb, but those who believe in the full expression of the Koran's "death to infidels" teaching.

When we were processing immigrants at Ellis Island during World War II, if we had opened an applicant's suitcase and found a dog-eared, underlined copy of *Mein Kampf,* no one would have called it racism for us to say, *No thanks!*

I don't think we'd let in members of a violent Nordic religion that believed in killing people who weren't blond and six foot two, although no such organization does exist, or would exist, outside of a Stieg Larsson novel.

But liberals had nothing else to say about Trump's plan except to call it "RACIST!"

On MSNBC, Chris Hayes called Trump's proposal "deeply dispiriting and disturbing" and also "fundamentally odious." Howard Dean called the idea "racist"—because foreign Muslims are the new blacks, and we have to make up for the legacy of slavery by bringing them here. The Democratic mayor of Philadelphia, Michael Nutter, said Trump had "taken a page from the playbook of Hitler" and was "literally trying to radicalize our fellow Americans against our American-Muslim and international Muslim brothers and sisters."[142]

Rachel Maddow began her discussion of Trump's proposed moratorium on Muslim immigration with this: "We never had an effective, well-organized national fascist party in this country." Rachel then quoted a slew of Republicans calling Trump a fascist. Steve Deace, a Salem Radio host, had tweeted that Trump's Muslim proposal was "creeping fascism." And the resident conservative at *The New York Times,* Ross Douthat, had written: "Trump may indeed be a little fascistic."[143]

None of them had the first idea what "fascism" means. Benito Mussolini adopted for his government the Roman symbol of fasces—a bundle of sticks—to signify strength in unity. He's bad because he allied with Hitler, not because he used a symbol of sticks. We have the same symbol on our Mercury dime. When people call someone a fascist, it's not a term of precise scientific meaning, but an epithet that's supposed to mean "Nazi." To say, "We never had an effective, well-organized national fascist party in this country" is no more meaningful than calling Trump a jerk.

Angry Muslims kept popping up on CNN and MSNBC to denounce Trump and complain about anti-Muslim bigotry in the United States. This country has taken in more than two million Muslims just since the 9/11 attack. If we don't make it three million, we're racists? If they'd prefer a country with more Muslims, why did they come here? These aren't Founding Father–generation Muslims. Sixty-three percent of Muslims in America are foreign-born,[144] so they had a choice. There are about fifty Muslim countries around the world—with no white devil oppressors!

Over on Fox News, Charles Krauthammer was beside himself, calling Trump's proposal "a terrible nightmare," "impulsive" "unreasonable," "truly, deeply bigoted," "indefensible."[145] In addition to those objections, Krauthammer demanded to know whether President Trump would frisk King Abdullah II of Jordan. Because absolute 100 percent consistency is the key to credibility! *If you're going to furlough a guy who passed bad checks, then you have to give one to a murderer. If you want a teaspoon of sugar in your coffee, you must want a pound.* No, there are gradations along a line.

This is how Republicans are tricked into saying stupid things and losing elections. Liberals never feel bound by a pointless pursuit of consistency. They support abortion for innocent babies but oppose the death penalty for heinous murderers. They're hysterical about Trump aide Corey Lewandowski grabbing a female reporter's arm but totally copacetic with Bill Clinton raping Juanita Broaddrick. Maybe what Trump would do is: suspend mass Muslim immigration—but also make exceptions! This is known as the fine art of making distinctions.

Megyn Kelly began her show the night of Trump's proposed

suspension of Muslim immigration with this: "Breaking tonight: The nation was hit by a terrorist attack less than seven days ago. For five days, the country and its press focused on the killers, trying to get to the bottom of who they were. How deeply connected to terror they had become. And who, if anyone, helped finance the plan or support their operation. On the sixth day, Donald Trump decided he'd like to get back into the media headlines."

Other Fox commentators were hopping mad that Trump had distracted from the important news of the day with a sideshow about Muslim immigration. Dana Perino complained, "No one knows how to step on a negative Obama news cycle better than Donald Trump." In case you didn't know: Obama had just given a *terrible* speech—a speech that "was largely panned." Greg Gutfeld agreed that Obama was about to "implode" over his speech about San Bernardino, until Trump off-roaded to something completely irrelevant: Muslim immigration.[146]

And when Fox News thinks Democrats are imploding, let me tell you, they are imploding. After three years of nonstop Benghazi coverage on Fox, the House of Representatives, led by Trey Gowdy, had recently brought in Hillary for her grilling. It was the moment all of Fox News had been dreaming of! The hearing accomplished the impossible: it made Hillary look presidential. According to polls, the Benghazi hearings convinced 72 percent of Americans, including a majority of Republicans, that there was nothing to Benghazi, and the committee was pursuing a political vendetta.[147] So if anyone knew how to take down the Democrats, it was Fox News. And then that oaf Trump stepped on an Obama speech "that was largely panned"!

The craziest argument against Trump's proposal was that admitting millions of Muslim immigrants was vital to our national security.

Obama's secretary of homeland security, Jeh Johnson, went on MSNBC to say that Trump's proposed Muslim ban, in addition to being "illegal, unconstitutional, and contrary to international law [and] un-American," would also "actually hurt our efforts at homeland security."[148]

Johnson's plan, announced a few days earlier, was to try extra hard to reach out to Muslims. "The overarching message to them is: Help us help you—help us to identify someone in your community who may be heading in the wrong direction, and how can we help you amplify the countermessage to the Islamic State message."[149]

On *Meet the Press,* Marco Rubio said that a pause in Muslim immigration was counterproductive, because "in order for us to identify homegrown violent extremism and prevent it or root it out before it takes action, we are going to need the cooperation of Muslim communities in this country."

> [*Frantically raising my hand*] Why don't we stop bringing in Muslims?
>
> *Well, we need to be nice to Muslims so they'll help us with all the Muslim terrorists we're bringing in!*
>
> Why are you bringing in Muslim terrorists?
>
> *I'm sorry, there will be no more questions.*

According to legions of national security experts interviewed on TV, Trump was "playing into ISIS's hands." It would actually *endanger* Americans to turn away immigrants like the ones who had just murdered fourteen Americans at the San Bernardino community center.

As Lester Holt said in the opening segment of *NBC Nightly News* that evening, "Security officials are raising the concern that the act of barring Muslims from entering this country would likely inspire more hostility toward the U.S., playing into the hands of ISIS, and ultimately put us in more danger."

They already seem pretty hostile.

Clinton defense secretary William Cohen said that Trump's proposal was "a message that ISIS actually wants us to spread so they can say, 'You see? We told you: this is really a clash of civilizations.'"[150]

Is that really what ISIS wanted? At least one of the Paris terrorists was known to have entered France as a "refugee," and ISIS had expressly announced that it was sneaking jihadist fighters into the West as refugees. Did they change their minds?

What wouldn't prove a "clash of civilizations"? According to national security experts, anything we did to oppose Islamic terrorism would "play into their hands," by proving this "clash." Prosecuting the guy who shot up the Army Recruiting Office in Chattanooga played into their hands. Imprisoning the Boston Marathon bomber played into their hands. Investigating Muslim immigrants for terrorist sympathies played into their hands.

How about exterminating ISIS?

Exterminating ISIS is exactly what they want!

But wouldn't that exterminate them?

Yes, but it would help their recruiting!

Evidently, the smart move was to fling open our borders, because that undermines their argument that we're anti-Muslim. Except we've already taken in a lot of Muslims, and they seem pretty bold and frisky now. Admitting two million Muslims since 9/11 hasn't stopped a lot of them from supporting ISIS. Then there's also the point that if we let them in, it will destroy our country. As we were learning, for some people, that's not a bug—it's a feature.

The media were in danger of overreaching. Their position was:

*Can you believe it—this guy Trump wants us to be proactive in pro-
tecting ourselves from terrorism?*

Amazed that voters were not deserting Trump in droves for
wanting to keep people who hate us out of our country, CNN political reporter Sara Murray explained, "Donald Trump does really
have this sort of sticky support among people who really do believe
what he says. People who are fearful, mistrustful, don't understand
the Muslim community."[151]

No, Sara, I think the issue is that Trump supporters *do* understand the Muslim community. "Fearful" and "mistrustful" are now
media code for "acting on basic human nature and common sense."

Republicans, in love with their own purity, expressed shock and
indignation at Trump's proposed Muslim ban.

Senator Marco Rubio called the idea "offensive and outlandish."

Jeb! said Trump was "unhinged."

Senator Lindsey Graham said, "Tell Donald Trump to go to
hell."[152]

*Vote for me—even if we experience a terrorist attack, we'll know
we did the right thing!*

RNC chair Reince Priebus said of Trump's policy, "I don't agree.
We need to aggressively take on radical Islamic terrorism, but not
at the expense of our American values."

House Speaker Paul Ryan said, "This is not conservatism. What
was proposed yesterday is not what this party stands for. And more
important, it's not what this country stands for."

Republican majority leader Senator Mitch McConnell said,
"Restricting Muslim travel to the United States . . . would be completely inconsistent with American values."

These guys might not have been the best spokesmen for "our
American values." Governors of more than two dozen states had
already announced that they would not accept any of the Syrian
"refugees." Exit polls showed that 70 percent of voters in the

Republican primaries agreed with Trump's Muslim ban, even in states that Trump didn't win, such as Texas and Wisconsin.[153]

And that's how many were willing to tell pollsters in face-to-face interviews that they agreed with Trump, after months of both Democrats and Republicans calling Trump's proposal "dangerous," "scapegoating," "offensive," akin to "Hitler," "fascism," and "absurd."[154] How many voters might approve of a Muslim ban in the privacy of a voting booth?

The night of Obama's January 2016 State of the Union address, all of official Washington stood up to oppose Trump's Muslim ban. Obama took shots at Trump from the podium, denouncing "any politics that targets people because of race or religion" as well as those who "insult Muslims." The only time House Speaker Ryan applauded Obama's speech was when he was sermonizing about Muslim immigration. We are never stronger than when we admit people who hate us!

South Carolina governor Nikki Haley gave the response to Obama's address, which should have counted as an in-kind donation to the Trump campaign. Having decided that the plutocrats' side on immigration hadn't been given a fair hearing, Haley regurgitated all the worst of the Paul Ryan/Eric Cantor/RNC open-border clichés.

- She said anyone who is "willing to work hard, abide by our laws, and love our traditions" is welcome in our country.

  No one who is "willing to work hard" can ever be turned away? That's the definition of open borders. After seven months of Trump, the GOP's big concession on immigration was: Okay, no more welfare layabouts.

- Haley said we should "fix our broken immigration system"—code for amnesty—by "welcoming properly vetted legal immigrants, regardless of religion."

  What exactly are we "vetting" if we can't look at religion?

- Referring to Trump, Haley dismissed "the loudest voice in the room," saying we should welcome all immigrants "just like we have for centuries."

    Has Haley read a history book? Calvin Coolidge shut down immigration for half a century.

- "The best thing we can do," Haley concluded, "is turn down the volume."

    Which is exactly what the GOP had been saying to voters for decades: you guys need to shut the hell up.

Had I been the deaf interpreter for Nikki's speech, I would have signed: "Hello, I'm Nikki Haley. For some bizarre reason, I was elected governor of South Carolina in 2010. Tonight I end my political career. Thank you. Goodnight."

Although everyone within five miles of a television greenroom was gasping in horror at Trump's Muslim ban, voters loved the idea. San Bernardino had finally jolted them. Muslims move to our country—and are they grateful? Not so you'd notice. They say, *Okay, now that we're here, you've got two choices: either convert or we kill you.* (But I love the plan of bringing millions more Muslims into our country. Some of them are bound to be sympathetic to us!)

While the media were frantically trying to persuade the public that Trump had revealed himself to be an incipient Adolf Hitler, the public kept trying to tell the media that they rather liked his idea to suspend Muslim immigration.

Both NBC News and CNN rushed to Trump rallies to get reactions from his supporters. Actual voters showed beatific calm at Trump's proposal, recognizing that he would not take the additional nine steps that only a paranoid psychotic would imagine, such as excluding the king of Jordan, creating a "religion registry," or barring the return of Muslim servicemen.

No one interviewed by CNN or NBC disagreed with Trump, and they were all lovely people. The first person NBC's Ali Vitali interviewed said, "I think that that is a very wise decision made very prudently after due diligence, and I'm impressed with the fact that he's bold enough to come out and do that." The next one said, "I think it's a good idea. With everything going on in the world right now—I mean, it sounds harsh, but reality is reality." It was the same for CNN. Correspondent Randi Kaye reported, "No one here we spoke with had a problem" with Trump's Muslim ban.

(Does TV need viewers? I wonder if it would help if *any* of their programming reflected the opinions of so many Americans?)

The Trump supporters interviewed by Kaye knew more about our immigration policies than she did. Lauren Martel called Trump's idea "very prudent," adding, "We have to protect our American citizens first, and the vetting process and the whole program lacks integrity."

Kaye then informed CNN viewers, "That's not true. In fact, the vetting process, run through multiple agencies, is vigorous." *Oh, boy, I feel stupid now.*

I don't know what Trump supporter Lauren Martel does for a living, but she knows more about the government's vetting process than CNN correspondents do. While the media insistently told us that the vetting of Syrian refugees was absolutely painstaking—you wouldn't believe the rectal probe they're getting!—their only evidence was the length of time it took.[155] Twenty-four months! *Waiting* is not *vetting*. Twenty-four months is the blink of an eye to people who can hold a grudge for a thousand years.

Just two months earlier, in October 2015, Michael Steinbach, assistant director of the FBI's counterterrorism division, had told Congress that in Syria, "all of the data sets—the police, the intel services—that normally you would go to seek information don't exist."[156] What exactly was being "vetted" during those grueling twenty-four months? There's no Syrian crime database. Syria barely has a phone book.[157] Our investigators can take fingerprints all day long, but if there's nothing to check the fingerprints against, then nothing has been "vetted."

It's possible that during that agonizing twenty-four months of waiting, someone might tip off our immigration officials about a particular applicant. Then our government would admit them anyway—as they did with the family of the Boston Marathon bombers, Tamerlan and Dzhokhar Tsarnaev.[158] The Russian government expressly warned both the CIA and the FBI that Tsarnaev family members were followers of radical Islam. Maybe Russia should call CNN's Randi Kaye directly next time, so she'll at least know as much as random South Carolinians attending a Trump rally.

A few weeks before the San Bernardino attack, the *National Journal*'s Ron Fournier claimed on Fox News, without contradiction, that "1.5 million refugees have come through this system since 2001—Middle East refugees, 1.5 million—and none of them have been terrorists." Bret Baier, Charles Krauthammer, and *The Washington Post*'s Robert Costa nodded thoughtfully.[159]

Here are some—and these are just the ones I happen to know about. In 2009, Waad Ramadan Alwan and Mohanad Shareef Hammadi were admitted to the United States from Iraq as "refugees." Within a few years, they were arrested in Bowling Green, Kentucky, for plotting terrorist acts in the United States. It turned out they'd both been part of the insurgency against Americans in Iraq. Alwan's fingerprints had actually been found on IEDs used against American troops.[160]

That's some careful vetting. Our government couldn't even figure out which Iraqis had helped Americans during the war and which were building IEDs to kill them.

Fazliddin Kurbanov was admitted as a refugee from Uzbekistan in 2009. Soon after arriving, he began communicating with the

Islamic Movement of Uzbekistan, telling them, "We are the closest ones to the infidels . . . What would you say if, with the help of God, we implement a martyrdom act?"[161] Investigators found ammonium nitrate, acetone, aluminum powder, and Tannerite in his apartment, which Kurbanov planned to use in bombing either a Boise park during Fourth of July celebrations or a U.S. military base.[162] Three months before Fox News viewers were being assured that no refugees had ever become terrorists, an Idaho jury convicted Kurbanov of a string of terrorism offenses. Now U.S. taxpayers will be paying his room and board for the next twenty-five years.

There's also the Boston Marathon bombers and Tamerlan's suspected co-conspirator in the throat-slitting of three Jews, Ibragim Todashev, who was carefully vetted and granted asylum. Years later, his father stated matter-of-factly, "He has nothing to fear . . . he would have faced no oppression."[163]

All were admitted after 9/11.

Then, two weeks after Fournier was assuring Fox viewers that not one terrorist had evaded the government's thorough vetting process, a Muslim immigrant on a marriage visa who'd been through "three extensive national security and criminal background screenings"[164] helped murder fourteen Americans in San Bernardino.

In early June 2016, we found out that a Somali war criminal had been working in airport security at Washington's Dulles Airport for the past few years—after having undergone "the full, federally mandated vetting process" and passing investigations by ICE, the FBI, and the TSA.[165]

And as we go to press, the largest mass shooting in U.S. history was just committed by a second-generation Muslim immigrant who'd been investigated by the FBI, twice, after co-workers reported him for claiming he was a member of terrorist organizations and hoped to commit a martyrdom act. He was also investigated by G4S, the private security firm that employed him as a security guard.

After the San Bernardino terrorist attack, *The New York Times* wearily explained that it was "impossible to conduct an exhaustive investigation for each of the tens of millions of people who are cleared each year to come to this country to work, visit or live."[166]

THEN DON'T ADMIT TEN MILLION PEOPLE A YEAR! Getting into the United States should be like getting into Harvard, with an admissions committee setting certain firm bars, such as: no criminal record, no low-skilled workers, no expensive medical conditions, and no fundamentalist Muslims.

When you get the kids a dog, do you look for a dog with cancer and a heart ailment, so he'll have to wear a diaper and be walked ten times a day? He wasn't born into the family. We can choose any dog we want. Why not get a dog who doesn't have these problems? Similarly, we can choose any immigrants we want. Why are we going out of our way to bring in people with endless problems?

America is under no obligation to solve the world's poverty problem, and the church ladies don't get to dictate what "we are" as Americans. If people want to run do-goody social service organizations, they should spend their own money. If it's our country, the subject at least deserves to be discussed out in the open. Most people will say, "God bless them, but we have to take care of our own." Americans are happy to do a few things, and we do a lot, but we don't need to keep taking in the terrorists, criminals, and welfare scammers from around the world.

Doesn't America have enough trouble? Some problems we have dropped on us and we have to deal with them. The legacy of slavery—right there, isn't that enough? We have our own criminals and psychotics. We've got earthquakes, tornadoes, and hurricanes. Why did we have to go looking for more problems to bring into our country? It's as if Mom went shopping and came home with a trunkful of trouble:

Aren't we fully stocked on trouble, honey?

I know, but I was at the store and they had such a
good sale going on—only $100 billion!

It's not as if there aren't cultures that are remarkably un-diverse—Japan, South Korea, Iceland, Denmark, Finland . . . One can't help but notice that they don't have certain problems that we do.

Americans keep being hectored to take "refugees" from terrorist-producing countries because to do otherwise would be "a betrayal of our values." Republicans, terrified of saying something that would get them in trouble with *The New York Times* editorial board, enthusiastically agree. Only Trump remembered another long-forgotten American value: protecting Americans.

We desperately needed a person of ordinary common sense to say, *Wait a minute, guys—why are we doing this?* The only one who would say it was Donald Trump.

CHAPTER TWELVE

So Close!
The Plan to Destroy America Was Almost Complete

One can't help but be impressed by the coolness and steadiness of the people controlling our media culture. *We just won't talk about immigration, and if we don't talk about it, it doesn't exist.* It's win-win-win for *The New York Times*: they get to be morally superior; change the electorate so that their side can win elections; and then claim that their editorials were vindicated. And they get cheap maids at the same time! The only people to suffer—and suffer a lot—are America's working class. *The Times* has been getting kind of sick of them anyway.

Until Trump, the elites had the whole thing wired. Under Obama, the government had been secretly moving thousands of Muslim refugees and Central American "children" to their communities, warning border agents, *You can't talk about this.*[167]

They didn't need to run this immigration scam forever, only until the Democrats have California-style majorities. Then they wouldn't have to worry about elections and could say, *Screw you. We did this deliberately.*

That's what happened in Britain. The Blair government secretly brought in millions of migrants, because the elites were bored with white-bread, boring British people and wanted to make Britain "multicultural"—all of which was exposed by award-winning investigative journalist Tom Bower in his 2016 book *Broken Vows: Tony Blair—The Tragedy of Power*.[168] A few years earlier, Blair speechwriter Andrew Neather revealed that the Labour Party had intentionally pushed through mass immigration from the third world, "to rub the Right's nose in diversity and render their arguments out of date."[169] Almost all of the more than two million third world migrants brought in under Blair are now British citizens.[170]

Throughout this process of replacement, the British media didn't make a peep. Even after three Pakistanis and one Jamaican committed a coordinated bombing of the London subways and buses on July 7, 2005, killing fifty-two people and injuring hundreds, anyone who raised questions about the rapid transformation of Britain would be dismissed as a "racist."[171] The BBC studiously avoided discussing immigration, just as the American media does—or did, until Trump.

The media were mostly mad that people found out about immigration. The transformation of America under Clinton, Bush, and especially Obama was proceeding as it had in Britain, with the media squelching any discussion of immigration—except to periodically inform us that millions of poverty-stricken, welfare-receiving immigrants are FANTASTIC for the economy.

In April 2013, Judicial Watch released e-mails proving that the U.S. Department of Agriculture was working hand in hand with the Mexican government to sign up illegal aliens for food stamps. A USDA official, Yibo Wood—pause on that name for a moment—had written, in Spanish, to the Mexican embassy, explaining: "**<u>You need not divulge information regarding your immigration status in seeking this benefit for your children</u>**,"—bold and underline, Yibo's.

No media outlet breathed a word about the documents, including Fox News. Two months later, congressional Democrats would block a farm bill because of proposed cuts to the food stamp program, which had mysteriously skyrocketed from $37.6 billion in 2008 to an astronomical $78.4 billion by 2012.[172]

It's almost a joke how the media hide true, relevant, and important information about immigration. This is how NBC News described New Hampshire's heroin epidemic, which is entirely a result of Mexican drug cartels streaming across our nonexistent border:[173] "With a population of roughly 1.4 million, the Granite State has one of the highest per-capita rates of addiction in the country. As the problem has worsened over the last decade, however, access to substance abuse treatment has not improved."[174]

Instead of worrying about treatment, how about preventing the drugs from coming in? No, we had to accept that drugs pouring in from Mexico is a fact of life. The only issue was how to help addicts after they were already addicted. If NBC were reporting on how the faulty manufacturing of some child's toy caused it to periodically explode and maim American children, would the rest of that sentence be "however, access to emergency room treatment has not improved"?

A person could have made a lot of money on bar bets by asking people basic facts about immigration, such as whether immigrants received more government assistance than natives (they do); whether immigrants get affirmative action over the native-born in college admissions and government programs (they do); whether America had taken in another two million Muslim immigrants since 9/11 (we have).

In the past half century, one-quarter of Mexico's entire population has moved to the U.S., every "homegrown" terrorist attack since 9/11 was committed by someone who was here as a result of

Teddy Kennedy's 1965 immigration act, and thousands of Americans are killed every year by immigrants. I guarantee you, the editor of *The New Yorker* knows none of these things.

So a lot of those "specifics" the media kept clamoring for had been missing from the immigration debate for some time. The average eight-year-old Guatemalan knew more about U.S. immigration policy than our media.

No one was talking about the cost to society of immigration, at all, B.T. (Before Trump). The media's only communiqués on the subject involved endless paeans to immigrants doing jobs "Americans won't do," creating jobs, paying taxes, and boosting our national GDP. A fuller version of those claims is: immigrants are doing jobs American did, until immigrants got here and drove down the wages; they're creating jobs, which they then give to their cousins; if they pay any taxes at all—which could only be sales taxes—they're consuming gigantically more in government services than they're paying; and their main contribution to the national economy is purchasing food, which they eat.

Forget the enormous costs of criminal immigrants—counted in addicted, overdosed, raped, and murdered Americans. The most hardworking, law-abiding immigrants impose enormous costs on society, while the alleged benefits go primarily to the immigrants themselves. Immigration may be good for the immigrants—and the minuscule number of Americans with servants—but it's a net loss for most Americans.

Take just one cost: education. According to the Department of Education, the country spends $12,401 a year for every child attending school, grades K through 12.[175] And that's the average cost, not the astronomically higher cost for a child who doesn't speak English. The highest combined state and local sales tax anywhere is 9.45 percent. So for America to break even on one illegal alien, with one child, the illegal would have to spend more than $124,000 on taxable goods every year. And that's assuming our imaginary illegal uses no other government services—no English translators, no food stamps, no earned-income tax credits, no subsidized housing, no Social Security benefits, no roads, no subways, no police, no hospitals, no libraries, no parks, and so on.

You can't say the media didn't make the case for open borders. No arrow was left sheathed. They had phony polls, Hispanic grievance groups, a lock on the entire media—including *The Wall Street Journal* and Fox News—both political parties, a Republican president from 2001 to 2009, the official Republican nominee for president in 2008, and a sitting Democratic president from 2009 to today. And they didn't care about looking stupid. The persistent demand for a "pathway to citizenship" (amnesty) to be granted simultaneously with vague promises about border security was like some con artist—*No, see, I need your wallet, because otherwise how will you know to trust me?*

In January 2013, the Republican "Hispanic Leadership Network" issued a diktat to elected Republicans, coaching them on which words and phrases they may and may not use.

The memo instructed:

- Do acknowledge that "Our current immigration system is broken and we need to fix it."
    Sounds tough, but commits you to nothing.
- Don't begin with "We are against amnesty."
    No need to make rash commitments that will only inhibit you later.
- Do use the phrase "earned legal status."
    Creates the impression that not everyone will get amnesty, but everyone will.
- Don't use the phrase "pathway to citizenship."
    Everyone knows it's more like a "teleporter to citizenship."

- Do use the wording "enforcement of our borders includes more border patrol, technology, and building a fence where it makes sense."

  Fools the rubes!

- Don't use phrases like "send them all back," "electric fence," "build a wall along the entire border."

  What are you, Pat Buchanan?

- Do use "undocumented immigrant" when referring to those here without documentation.

  We also like Rand Paul's "undocumented Americans."

- Don't use the word "illegals" or "aliens." Don't use the term "anchor baby."

  Even we can't defend you if you do.

- Do acknowledge that President Obama broke his promise and failed to propose any immigration reform for five years, while using this issue as a political wedge.

  Immigration reform is a Republican idea!

- Do talk about the issues you support like overhauling the bureaucratic visa system, creating a viable temporary worker program, a workable e-verify system, and border security.

  Helpful in eating up time. No one will notice when you don't do it.

- Don't focus on amnesty as a tenet of immigration reform.

  They don't need to know that.

- Don't use President Reagan's immigration reform as an example applicable today.[176]

  No need to remind everyone that we've done this before.

They forgot the part about not hitting each other with their pocketbooks when angry.

Other Republicans slavishly followed the Hispanic Leadership Network's directions. Trump proceeded to violate every rule—as well as a few new ones.

ANGRY WHITE MEDIA REFUSE TO MENTION I-WORD (NOT ISIS!)

When Trump launched his campaign with a bracingly politically incorrect speech about illegal immigration from Mexico, neither the liberal nor "conservative" media could forgive him. Americans weren't supposed to find out that they were being replaced with foreigners to benefit the rich. The Republican Brain Trust had no choice: it would have to destroy Trump as an example to the others.

The day of Trump's announcement, guest host Doug McKelway on Fox's hard news program *Special Report* described Trump as "often a punch line," adding that "some" were dismissing his candidacy "as a stunt." For balance, McKelway added that Trump also has a huge "ego" and "lack of experience."[177] He then read aloud from the Democratic National Committee press release mocking Trump.[178] (The mysterious "some" who were dismissing Trump's run as a "stunt" evidently included the head of Fox News.)

Panelist Charles Krauthammer commented that it would be "analytical overkill to parse the actual things" Trump said, calling his speech a "stream of consciousness" that was premised on "xenophobia." For the opposing view, George Will said Trump had a big mouth and was a "rich megalomaniac," "an Edsel," and "very injurious to the Republican Party."[179]

Will also sneered at Trump for complaining about illegal immigration, because "the immigration of Mexicans has been for at least five years either zero or negative. I don't know where Mr. Trump has been."[180] This alleged fact is an article of faith at *The Huffington Post* but it is quite vigorously contested by people who actually know something, such as U.S. border guards and the U.S. Census.[181] Most people would go with the Census and Border Patrol.

Months later, Fox News' Charles Krauthammer was still sputtering about Trump's outlandish proposal to enforce immigration laws. *You mean, sir, if I understand Trump correctly, laws on the books—we should enforce them?*

Krauthammer said Trump's proposal to deport illegals was not only infeasible but "fundamentally un-American": "The deportation of eleven million people—which would be the largest police action in the United States since the rounding up of Japanese Americans in the Second World War—is not a reasonable proposal. It's a disgrace."[182] (Author's note: ILLEGALS ARE NOT "AMERICANS"!)

What other efforts to enforce the law are "fundamentally un-American"? When illegality reaches a critical mass, is any attempt at enforcement not only impractical but un-American? Does that apply to tax cheats? With the immigrants we're bringing in, not paying taxes is about to reach Grecian proportions. How about speeders? If enough people start going 180 miles per hour on I-95, is it "disgraceful" and "un-American" to pull them over?

At least Trump's immigration policies had finally brought MSNBC, CNN, and Fox News together with the harmony of a common purpose: Stop Trump!

Instead of admitting that they were depressed about the success of Trump's immigration proposals, the media mostly tried pretending Trump hadn't mentioned immigration at all. It was all his attitude! Yes, that was it. Voters were in an anti-establishment mood. They were angry. Not about anything in particular. Political analysts would sooner praise Sarah Palin's speaking style than mention Trump's signature issue. It was as if they were writing election pieces from Mars.

Political savants took to psychoanalyzing the sort of person who would support Trump. *New York Times* columnist David Brooks, quoting *Commentary*'s Peter Wehner, described the typical Trump supporter as someone who is "longing to return to the past and is fearful of the future ... characterized by resentments and grievances, by distress and dismay."[183] In *The Miami Herald,* John Lantigua—a two-time winner of the Robert F. Kennedy Journalism Award—wrote that the country's "rapidly changing demographics" had allowed Trump to tap into voters' "insecurity, fear ... xenophobia."[184] And on *Vox,* Amanda Taub wrote that "rising diversity" was threatening to Trump voters, taking away their sense of the "familiar, orderly, secure—and replac[ing] it with something that feels scary."[185]

We get where you're coming from, David, Peter, John, and Amanda. You're afraid. The world is changing. It's hard to clean your apartment, and Hispanics are so docile, so loving—like Labradors. They happily work for $7 an hour, and when Rosa is done with the bathtub you could eat off it!

Without Rosa, who would you hire? An American? *A black person*? Deep anxieties triggered there. Hispanics are so much more tractable. And if you hired a white maid to clean your toilets—it's so humiliating for them! Do you think you're better than they are? We get that. Honestly, we are sympathetic. That's just not enough of a reason to change our culture and wreck our country. Request denied.

Liberals love to sneer at ordinary people's "nativism," for minding when their neighborhoods become places where no one speaks English, but would it bother *New York Times* readers if their schools were inundated with people who talked like Sarah Palin and their kids came home from school saying "You betcha"?

In 2006, *The Los Angeles Times'* Sam Quinones previewed the new country our politicians were designing for us, in a story about a Mexican illegal immigrant, Angela Magdaleno, who had just given birth to quadruplets.[186] That made it ten anchor babies for Angela and her husband, Alfredo Anzaldo, also an illegal, who had three additional children with two other women.

Unfortunately, Alfredo was unable to support his wife and thirteen children on a maximum salary of $400 a week as a carpet installer. Nonetheless, before the quadruplets, Angela had given birth to triplets, at age thirty-six, after undergoing an operation to reverse her tubal ligation and taking gargantuan amounts of fertility drugs—because her husband wanted a son.

The U.S. taxpayer was on the hook for not only free school lunches and $700 a month in Social Security payments and subsidized housing, but also Medi-Cal—which paid 100 percent of the health care needs of this enormous and very pricey family. Four of Angela's anchor babies were born underweight, one with hydrocephalus. The hydrocephalic child had already undergone three taxpayer-funded brain operations "and will require several more." Angela said, "I thank this country that they gave me Medi-Cal. There's nothing like that in Mexico."

Neither Angela nor Alfredo spoke English, despite having lived in this country for twenty-two and twenty-eight years, respectively. Nor did their teenage children.

Two of Angela's illegal alien sisters—out of ten siblings in the country illegally—had already fled California for Lexington, Kentucky, because—I quote—there were "fewer Mexicans there." The sister Alejandra raved about Kentucky, saying, "We're in a state where there's nothing but Americans." She noted the clean streets, police presence, and lack of gang activity. In California, she complained, "everyone thinks like in Mexico."

That was in 2006. Two years later:

DRAMATIC INCREASE OF
IMMIGRANTS IN KENTUCKY

Police tell us that the Latin Kings, Surenos and MS-13 gangs, all with ties to the Mexican Mafia are operating criminal enterprises in Kentucky. Cells have been identified in Shelbyville, Louisville and Lexington. A narcotics officer told us some illegals have wired 15,000 dollars a week for months to cartels in Mexico.

[Shelbyville city councilman] Shane Sutter said, "We don't have a swat team. We don't have a gang task force. We're just a small town.[187]

When Trump started talking about anchor babies, the entire media needed smelling salts, ending with this exchange with ABC's Tom Llamas:

LLAMAS: That's an offensive term. People find that hurtful.
TRUMP: You mean it's not politically correct, and yet everybody uses it? . . .
LLAMAS: Look it up in the dictionary—it's offensive.
TRUMP: I'll use the word "anchor baby." Excuse me, I'll use the word "anchor baby."

That's when we discovered that if Republicans don't immediately go prostrate and grovel for failing to adhere to *The Nation* magazine's stylebook, the word police don't have a "plan B."

At the second Republican debate, CNN's Jake Tapper pulled off the amazing feat of asking Trump about his opposition to anchor babies without using the term "anchor babies." Instead, Tapper claimed to be asking about "birthright citizenship." Say—here's one of those "specifics" journalists are always hankering for: "birthright citizenship" is something completely different from "anchor babies." Birthright citizenship means that children born in the United States to legal immigrants are citizens, which has been the law since 1898.

Anchor babies are born to illegal immigrants. Those children were never considered citizens until Supreme Court Justice

William Brennan made it up in 1982 and slipped it into a footnote. They're called anchor babies because it is the child's alleged citizenship—invented in 1982—that "anchors" the entire illegal alien family here, including cousins and elderly grandparents, collecting government benefits for the rest of their lives. There's nothing offensive about the term—it's not racial or sexual. It's a boating metaphor.

In any event, Tapper asked Trump to respond to Fiorina's claim that his attack on "birthright citizenship" (anchor babies) was "pandering" and nothing could be done about it.

Trump said: "Well, first of all, the Fourteenth Amendment says very, very clearly to a lot of great legal scholars . . . [that] it can be corrected with an act of Congress, probably doesn't even need that. A woman gets pregnant. She's nine months, she walks across the border, she has the baby in the United States, and we take care of the baby for eighty-five years. I don't think so. . . . And by the way, this is not just with respect to Mexico. They are coming from Asia to have babies here, and all of a sudden we have to take care of the babies for the life of the baby."

After a fair bit of gibbering by Fiorina—"You can't just wave your hands and say the Fourteenth Amendment is gonna go away"—the dispute ended this way:

> TRUMP: I believe that a reading of the Fourteenth Amendment allows you to have an interpretation where this is not legal and where it can't be done. I've seen both sides, but some of the greatest scholars agree with me. . . .
> FIORINA: But you—you would stipulate, Mr. Trump, but not everyone agrees with you.
> TRUMP: That's true, sure.[188]

Ten minutes of the debate for Fiorina to make the scintillating point "Not everyone agrees with you."

Liberals want mass third world immigration because as soon as they have invincible Democratic majorities, utopia will arrive. Then they're not going to return the GOP's phone calls—just like in California.

The GOP had a different set of reasons for supporting mass immigration: the business community wants cheap labor. Not every member of the donor class derives a benefit from mass immigration, but no rich person is willing to become a hate figure by bankrolling the opposition. Republican officeholders ran the numbers and realized the electoral implications won't be felt for a few years, and by then they'll be retired. *Après moi, le déluge.*

Even if everything else about the cool calculations to destroy our country were not obnoxious, where do they get the right to do this?

Do not imagine this is being done by accident or laziness. The open-borders crowd has been very deliberate, very careful. *We aren't going to ask ordinary people what they think. We're just going to do this because we think we're right, and at certain point it will be impossible to change it back.*

Republican politicians know damn well that voters want less immigration. Otherwise they wouldn't lie and promise to secure the borders when they need our votes. They just never do it.

Trump is the only frontal assault that will work.

CHAPTER THIRTEEN

Trump Builds Wall, Makes GOP Pay for It

Without Trump in the race, we have some idea what the campaign would have looked like, and it wouldn't have been about a wall, anchor babies, sanctuary cities, or a temporary Muslim ban.

The first question, at the first GOP debate—after the free-for-all about the pledge to support the eventual nominee—was this:

> MEGYN KELLY: Gentlemen, our first round of questions is on the subject of electability in the general election, and we start tonight with you, Dr. Carson. You are a successful neurosurgeon, but you admit that you have had to study up on foreign policy, saying there's a lot to learn. Your critics say that your inexperience shows. *You've suggested that the Baltic states are not a part of NATO, just months ago you were unfamiliar with the major political parties and government in Israel, and . . . zzzzzzzzzzzzzzzzzz.*

At the second debate, Ted Cruz said there was "no more important topic" in the 2016 election than the Iran deal.

The voters pretty clearly vetoed that idea. Although we were all looking forward to a spirited competition among Republicans to see who could express the most disgust for the Iran deal, Americans responded, *Yes, that's very important, Ted—we're going to get to it real soon, but first we're going to build a wall.*

Trump's first interview the day he announced was on Fox News' *O'Reilly Factor*. Bill O'Reilly's first question was: "ISIS. How are you going to defeat ISIS?"[189] He then spent two-thirds of the interview asking Trump about Iraq, Syria, Iran, and Putin. Nothing about immigration—other than O'Reilly's scoffing at the idea that Mexico would pay for the wall.

One month later, O'Reilly introduced a segment with Trump saying this: "Problems like illegal immigration are not being dealt with effectively. That is the reason Donald Trump's campaign has caught fire: anger. Last Friday about thirty thousand people showed up to hear Donald Trump speak in Alabama . . ."[190]

While the other candidates were memorizing all the countries in NATO, practicing their pronunciations of Arabic names, and learning the geography of Syria, Trump shot to the top of the polls with an opening speech about Mexico sending rapists and drugs to our country. *Do not mistake me for a politician of nuance; I'm going to tell the truth.*

What if, instead of talking about Mexican rapists and a wall, Trump's opening speech had been about how "Cuban exiles . . . former slaves and refugees . . . together built the freest and most prosperous nation ever"? Or suppose his plan for "good-paying modern jobs" hadn't been to stop dumping low-wage workers on the country, but to update our higher education system? And imagine if Trump had said that America's prosperity depended on our making "the world more stable"?

Is that the guy who was going to rocket to the top of the polls? Because that was golden boy Marco Rubio's opening speech, give or take a few clichés about "the new American century."

Governor Scott Walker was still talking about his honor in attending "Badger Boys State" and representing Wisconsin at "Boys Nation" at about the same point in his announcement speech when Trump was telling his audience: "When Mexico sends its people, they're not sending their best. They're not sending you. They're not sending you. They're sending people that have lots of problems, and they're bringing those problems with them. They're bringing drugs. They're bringing crime. They're rapists. And some, I assume, are good people."

Suppose—like Walker—Trump hadn't mentioned immigration at all. What if he had instead proposed a slew of new military interventions? Who doesn't like military interventions?

Walker's opening speech included these demands:

> "We need to stop the aggression of Russia into sovereign nations."

> "We need to stop China's . . . territorial expansion into international waters and speak out about their abysmal human rights record."

> "We need to have the capacity to protect our national security interests—here and abroad—and those of our allies."

Is that the candidate who was going to win more votes in a presidential primary than any Republican in history?

Trump's crafty strategy was to push policies that were wildly popular with voters but that the two parties and the media had a gentlemen's agreement never to discuss, primarily immigration.

It wasn't that hard to break out of the pack. Trump's position on immigration was totally antithetical to that of the Republican National Committee, all the Washington think tanks, at least two-thirds of Republican officeholders, the party's unofficial cable news network—Fox News—and 99 percent of GOP donors. On the other hand, Trump's positions happened to be supported by the vast majority of Republican voters and at least a fifth of Democrats.

For nearly twenty years, the voters have been begging for an end to illegal immigration—and a pretty steep cut in legal immigration, while we're at it. But Washington wouldn't listen.

These were the soil conditions for the growth of the Trump vegetable:

- In 2005, Senator John McCain pushed an amnesty bill with Teddy Kennedy. Public opposition to the bill shut down the congressional switchboard.

- In 2006, President Bush launched his campaign for amnesty. It was so violently opposed by voters—polls showed it was less popular than the Iraq War[191]—that Bush's party was wiped out in the midterm elections that year, giving Democrats huge majorities in both the House and the Senate.

- In 2013, Tea Party favorite Marco Rubio pushed an amnesty bill through the U.S. Senate. Three years later, he ran for president and, despite having Fox News as his super PAC, was slaughtered in his own state by a New York City developer who said he'd build a wall and deport illegals.

- In 2014, House majority leader Eric Cantor became the first member of leadership ever to lose his seat in a primary, after being walloped by an unknown economics professor who ran against him on his support for amnesty.[192] Cantor had gotten fantastic press for pushing a "Dreamers" act that would grant amnesty to illegal alien children, claiming incomprehensibly, that "one of the great founding principles of our country was that children would not be punished for the mistakes of their parents."[193] Wasn't that the rallying cry at Valley Forge?

- In the 2014 midterm elections, voters gave Republicans one more chance. Senator Mitch McConnell promised to block Obama's "executive amnesty," if only the GOP was handed a Senate majority. The voters complied. Surely politicians had noticed what had happened to Eric Cantor and wouldn't lie to the voters again. The GOP won sweeping majorities in both houses of Congress.

And Republicans betrayed them, once again.

It was a stunning double cross. Unlike GOP promises to repeal Obamacare, defunding Obama's unconstitutional "executive amnesty" was easy. Even if Obama were to veto a Department of Homeland Security spending bill, 200,000 out of 230,000 employees were "essential" and would be required to stay on the job. There would be no closures of museums, no national park shutdowns, no Social Security checks unmailed. The media would scream and blame Republicans—but at some point in their stories, they'd have to mention what the fight was about: Obama's widely hated "executive amnesty." Instead, Republicans caved and allowed Obama to use taxpayer money for a program in express violation of federal law, implemented in violation of the Constitution.

On Fox News, George Will praised the betrayal, saying the Republican Senate was merely exercising "adult supervision."

The country exploded in rage. What was it going to take? What other laws would our elected representatives decide to flout? The country was looking at complete chaos if the president, with the connivance of Congress, could ignore federal law. Really, *really* wanting open borders isn't an excuse to be issuing Mussolini-like fiats.

They couldn't learn.

When Trump said, at the first debate, "If it weren't for me, you wouldn't even be talking about illegal immigration," Carly Fiorina was not on the debate stage. She had to wait until she'd bullied her way into the second debate to say, "Immigration did not come up in 2016 because Mr. Trump brought it up. We talked about it in 2012, we talked about it in 2008. We talked about it in 2004. We have been talking about it for twenty-five years. This is why people are tired of politicians."

She then proceeded to talk about it in the exact same way politicians have been talking about it for twenty-five years. The only cliché Fiorina missed was the one where you cite your immigrant relatives.

Her answer was not only the same one Republicans had been giving forever; but nearly word for word, the answer Obama had given when he was running for president in 2008.

> OBAMA: I would say that they're justified in feeling frustrated because this administration, the Bush administration, has done nothing to control the problem that we have. We've had five million undocumented workers come over the borders since George Bush took office. It has become an extraordinary problem. The reason the American people are concerned is because they are seeing their own economic positions slip away. . . . Now, I have already stated that as president I will make sure that we finally have the kind of border security that we need.[194]

Politicians' usual pretend solutions—"border security that we need"—were: technology, "boots on the ground," and drones. What would any of those accomplish, exactly? Were the troops going to shoot illegals? Would the drones drop bombs on them? Or were we going to use the drones to watch illegals pouring into our country? If we can't stop them, I guess we may as well entertain ourselves.

How about some kind of, I don't know, permanent barrier that sits there, day and night, without needing to eat or sleep or collect a salary? Politicians opposed a wall not because they thought it wouldn't work, but because they knew it would.

SIDEBAR: IMMIGRATION GLOSSARY

"Our immigration system is broken": Wants amnesty

"Earned legal status": Wants amnesty

"Path to citizenship": Wants amnesty

"Back taxes": Wants amnesty

"Drones!": Wants amnesty

"I oppose amnesty": Wants amnesty

B.T.—Before Trump—we were more likely to get great ideas like this one from Jon Huntsman: "I hope that all of us, as we deal with this immigration issue, will always see it as an issue that revolves around real human beings." *Why, thank you, Governor! You've really thrown the debate wide open and given us all food for thought.*

Trump was the first presidential candidate to ask: Are our immigration policies good for the people who live here?

When asked to discuss immigration B.T., Republicans had precisely five talking points:

1. Cite your immigrant relatives.
2. Blame "Washington" for not "solving the problem."
3. Claim you support a "secure border."
4. Say that nothing will work.
5. Propose fake solutions that definitely won't work.

Here are examples of the honking immigration clichés from GOP candidates in the 2012 and 2016 races. These were said during televised debates, so they knew people were watching.

I HAVE RELATIVES WHO ARE IMMIGRANTS!

ROMNEY: My father was born in Mexico. My wife's father was born in Wales.[195]

HUNTSMAN: I have two daughters that came to this country—one from China, one from India—legally. I see this issue through their eyes.[196]

RICK SANTORUM: Look, I'm the son of an Italian immigrant.[197]

CRUZ: I am the son of an Irish-Italian mom and a Cuban immigrant dad.[198]

RUBIO: My family's immigrants. My neighbors are all immigrants. My in-laws are all immigrants.[199]

I BLAME WASHINGTON

NEWT GINGRICH: [Obama] failed to get any immigration reform through when he controlled the Senate and he controlled the House. He could ram through "Obamacare," but he couldn't deal with immigration.[200]

HUNTSMAN: The thing we need to do most on illegal immigration, because there has been zero leadership in Washington—and with zero leadership in Washington, we've created this patchwork of solutions.[201]

FIORINA: I would ask your audience at home to ask a very basic question: Why have Democrats not solved this problem? President Obama campaigned in 2007 and 2008 on solving the immigration problem. . . . Instead, he chose to do nothing.[202]

BUSH: Washington is holding us back. [We have] a broken immigration system that has been politicized rather than turning it into an economic driver.[203]

I WILL SECURE THE BORDER!

RON PAUL: I do think we should deal with our borders.[204]

SANTORUM: I believe that we need to secure the border.[205]

BUSH: Clearly, we need to secure the border.[206]

WALKER: I believe we need to secure the border. I've been to the border.[207]

CHRISTIE: What we need to do is to secure our border.[208]

RUBIO: When I'm president of the United States, before we do anything on immigration, we are going to secure the border.[209]

NOTHING WILL WORK

RON PAUL: Sure, we can secure the borders. A barbed-wire fence with machine guns—that would do the trick. I don't believe that's what America is all about. I just really don't.[210]

GINGRICH: We're not—we as a nation are not going to walk into some family . . . We're not going to walk in there and grab a grandmother out and then kick them out.[211]

BUSH: But to build a wall, and to deport people . . . It would destroy community life, it would tear families apart.[212]

RUBIO: I also believe we need a fence. The problem is if El Chapo builds a tunnel under the fence . . .[213]

INSTEAD, HOW ABOUT SOME
UTTERLY POINTLESS MEASURES?

HUNTSMAN: Secure the border. Eight hundred miles—we've got a third of it done between fencing and technology and National Guard boots on the ground.

RICK PERRY: Well, the first thing you need to do is have boots on the ground.[214]

FIORINA: Look, we know what it takes to secure a border.
We've heard a lot of great ideas here: money, manpower,
technology . . .[215]

CHRISTIE: We need to use electronics, we need to use drones,
we need to use FBI, DEA, and ATF . . .

GOOD FENCES MAKE GOOD NEIGHBORS—ESPECIALLY IF THE NEIGHBORS ARE CHILD-RAPING DRUG DEALERS.

No Republican candidate for president had ever said anything like this before: "I would build a great wall—and nobody builds walls better than me, believe me, and I'll build them very inexpensively. I will build a great, great wall on our southern border. And I will have Mexico pay for that wall. Mark my words."

Everyone said it was impossible. *How would a successful New York developer build something as inconceivably difficult as a wall?*

Trump provided specifications:

"So you take precast plank. It comes thirty feet long, forty feet long, fifty feet long. You see the highways where they can span fifty, sixty feet, even longer than that, right? And you do a beautiful, nice precast plank with beautiful everything. Just perfect. I want it to be so beautiful, because maybe someday they'll call it the Trump Wall. Maybe. So I have to make sure it's beautiful, right? I'll be very proud of that wall. If they call it the Trump Wall, it has to be beautiful. And you put that plank up and you dig your footings. And you put that plank up—there's no ladder going over that. If they ever go up there, they're in trouble, because there's no way to get down."[216]

What were the rest of them going to do about the border? Say,

"People are frustrated" and call for "border security," meaning: *You're never getting a wall, America.*

At least Jeb! didn't lie to us. He took the position that voters would respect him for not being one of those sleazy politicians who would give us false hope. Illegal immigration, he told voters, was an "act of love." He was like a dad explaining to his kid, *No you can't have the car. Maybe you'll understand why when you're older.*

Jeb! cited Reagan's optimism as a reason to dissolve America's borders, saying at one of the debates, "Are we going to take the Reagan approach, the hopeful, optimistic approach, the approach that says that you come to our country legally, you pursue your dreams with a vengeance, you create opportunities for all of us? Or the Donald Trump approach?"

Jeb! certainly was optimistic! The very day of that debate, ICE issued a press release announcing the deportation of an illegal alien who had raped a fourteen-year-old to death, then killed the girl's father.[217]

Despite the fact that Jeb! had been a successful governor of the third-largest state, had loads of impressive endorsements and the admiration of Rupert Murdoch, and started with more than $100 million in his war chest, Jeb! won only four delegates and was forced to drop out after South Carolina.

Apparently, voters preferred the Trump approach. Asked at a debate about his mad idea to build a wall, Trump said: "Correct. First of all, I want to build a wall, a wall that works. So important, and that's a big part of it. Second of all, we have a lot of really bad dudes in this country from outside . . . They go. If I get elected, first day, they're gone. Gangs all over the place. Chicago, Baltimore, no matter where you look. . . . So we have a country of laws. They're going to go out, and they'll come back if they deserve to come back. If they've had a bad record, if they've been arrested, if they've been in jail, they're never coming back. We're going to have a country again. Right now, we don't have a country, we don't have a border, and we're going to do something about it."

It took ten years, but on June 1, 2016, *The New York Times* finally admitted: "Support for immigration 'may be greatly overestimated.'"[218]

Imagine you live in a bad neighborhood where your house keeps getting broken into. You call up various fence companies to get an estimate; the salesmen come to your house and tell you this:

CONTRACTOR NO. 1: *We need to be much more strategic on how we deal with fencing, home security . . . There's much to do. And I think, rather than talking about this, which other fence companies have done, I hope to be that contractor, will fix this once and for all so that we can turn this into a driver for your safety.*

CONTRACTOR NO. 2: *You are hitting a nerve. You are. You are hitting a nerve. Your wife is frustrated. She's fed up. She doesn't think the backyard is working for her. And for contractors that want to just tune you out, they're making a mistake. Now, you've got your solutions; some of us have other solutions. You know, look, I balanced my household budget and ran a paper route when I was sixteen years old—*

YOU: Respectfully, can we talk about the fence?

CONTRACTOR NO. 2: *The point is that we all have solutions. You are touching a nerve because your family wants the fence to be built. They want to see an end to burglaries. They want to see it, and we all do. But we all have different ways of getting there. And you're going to hear from all the contractors about what our ideas are.*

CONTRACTOR NO. 3: *Let me set the record straight on a couple of things. The first is: the evidence is now clear that the majority of burglars are not from this neighborhood.*

*They're coming from the other side of town and neighboring
towns. Those places are the source of the people breaking
into your house, its majority.*

*I also believe you need a fence. The problem is if burglars
climb over the fence, we have to be able to deal with that,
too. And that's why you need to put your wife's jewelry in a
safe-deposit box and get a lockbox for your guns and all
sorts of other things to prevent burglaries. But I agree with
what you just said. People are frustrated.*

DONALD TRUMP CONTRACTING INC.: *I will build a great, great
wall around your yard. And I will have the burglars pay for
that wall.*

Those are exact paraphrases of what Jeb!, Kasich, and Rubio
said at the first debate, and of what Trump said about a wall in his
announcement speech.[219]

Who are you hiring?

Trump's closest competitor, Ted Cruz, was the only rival smart
enough to adopt nearly all of Trump's positions on immigration.
Between them, they won 80 percent of the vote in a multiple-
candidate field, until Cruz suspended his campaign in April.

It is no longer a question of what the party wants. The combined
vote for Trump and Cruz is a ringing chorus of what this party
wants: a wall, deportation, and a lot less immigration, especially
from Muslim countries. In other words, what the party wants is the
diametric opposite of what Washington wants. One would search
the history books in vain to find a party establishment so emphati-
cally rejected by the voters as the Republican Party was in 2016.

They want to keep the country. They want Trump.

CHAPTER FOURTEEN

The New Trumpian Party!

No matter how obvious it was that Trump was a runaway hit with voters, the GOP couldn't drop its smug cluelessness. By talking about Mexican rapists, the drug cartels, anchor babies, Kate Steinle, sanctuary cities, and a temporary ban on Muslim immigration, Trump shot to the top of the polls and, except for an aberrational poll or two, stayed there until, by early May, he had already won more presidential primary votes than any Republican in history.

The Weekly Standard marked the occasion by publishing a ten-million-word article explaining that the real problem with the Republican Party was its failure to lead on issues like ... farm subsidies and medical device payouts![220] Never has a political party been so severed from anything anyone cares about.

After ten months of venomous sneering from the entire Republican Brain Trust—every political consultant, pollster, and Beltway insider, Fox News, *National Review,* talk radio hosts Mark Levin and Glenn Beck—*The New York Times* reported that "Republicans have ruefully acknowledged that they came to this dire pass in no small part because of their own passivity."[221]

Their own "passivity." This is how people brag about how

admirable they are by pretending to apologize: *We screwed up; we were too nice.* What they're really saying is that they didn't screw up at all. They're just super people.

Checking my notes, I see that in the first few weeks after Trump announced, his rivals called him a "cancer on conservatism" (Rick Perry), "unhinged" (Jeb!), "sophomoric" (Rand Paul), and "a complete idiot . . . a race-baiting, xenophobic religious bigot . . . I don't think he has a clue about anything . . . Tell Donald Trump to go to hell . . . He's the world's biggest jackass" (Lindsey Graham). And that was before Marco Rubio got into Trump's penis size.

What do Republicans do when they're being aggressive?

Every few weeks we'd hear about a "turning point" with the media *finally* getting tough on Trump. He'd be attacked from every media outlet, go up in the polls, and then a week later we'd hear about another "turning point" in the media's coverage of Trump. (For variety, sometimes the media were "turning a corner.") Approximately every other week since he announced has been called "Trump's worst week yet!"

One turning point—out of a cast of thousands—came in November 2015, when *The Wall Street Journal* reported a "turning point" in the GOP's battle against Trump, with two super PACs planning ads expressly dedicated to attacking Trump, and a "well-connected GOP operative planning a 'guerrilla campaign' backed by secret donors to 'defeat and destroy'" him.[222] If only the GOP had shown that sort of vim in fighting Obama.

The attacks on Trump were relentless and bipartisan, full of Washington Republicans wailing that he'd be the end of the GOP, side by side with surveys of Democrats, praying for Trump but afraid of Rubio! No one, not even Sarah Palin, was ever subjected to as much contempt as Trump—he's a clown, an idiot, a buffoon! These Tourette syndrome attacks always included fiery denunciations of Trump for calling people names.

Shell-shocked by Trump's sweep of the primaries, party leaders set about trying to erect barriers to make sure something like this would never happen again. The party was "going so far," *The New York Times* reported, "as to consider diluting the traditional status of Iowa, New Hampshire and South Carolina as gatekeepers to the presidency."[223] The RNC seems to think Trump's nomination reflected some sort of mechanical defect, and, with a little tinkering, they can create a new kind of plasterboard that will withstand a nuclear explosion.

In addition to it being a wonderful thing that Trump is the Republican nominee, it was entirely predictable, given basic meteorological truths. It will happen every single time a candidate runs on popular issues both parties are ignoring, such as, off the top of my head: *Building a wall.*

It's really not that much of a mystery why everything the media thought was going to kill Trump made him more popular. The whole secret of the Trump campaign is that he tacked his sailboat into the wind, and the mother lode of votes went deeper than anyone ever imagined. He wins in the privacy of a voting booth, where even the most status-conscious, terrified-of-looking-Walmarty voters can say, *Screw it—no one will ever know.*

Trump's candidacy will be studied for the next hundred years at places like the Harvard Kennedy School. The GOP either will follow his lead and end up a better, stronger party, or it will go the way of the Whigs. And the cause will be the same: some people's need for cheap labor.

Jeb! thought he had it all sewn up with that $100 million war chest and a family that imagines it is wildly charismatic and beloved by all Americans. Rubio had the entire Fox News Network pulling for him every minute of every day. Ted Cruz had evangelical leaders, almost as much money as Jeb!, and data mining to rival Obama's operation.

Then Trump came along, like Groucho Marx offending all the stuck-up ladies as he sashayed through the party, dropping his cigar ash. And the voters said: WE CAN'T WAIT! WE'RE GOING TO BE LIVING IN AMERICA AGAIN!

APPENDIX

Geniuses

If you're General George Custer, it's one thing not to hear the distant hoofbeat, and quite another not to know when there's an arrow in your head.

> "Trump has a better chance of cameoing in another *Home Alone* movie with Macaulay Culkin—or playing in the NBA Finals—than winning the Republican nomination."
>
> —Harry Enten, "Why Donald Trump Isn't a Real Candidate, in One Chart," FiveThirtyEight, June 16, 2015

> "[Trump] doesn't expect to win the White House. The only thing he's selling is an image-enhancing candidacy for the presidency."
>
> —Jack Shafer, "Welcome to the Donald Trump Show," *Politico*, June 16, 2015

"The reality that he's in ninth place in the Republican field and my guess is [that he] probably won't ever crack the top five or six.... [Trump will have to] find some way to bow out of this race at some point while at least, in his mind, saving face."

> —McKay Coppins, political writer for *BuzzFeed*, MSNBC's *All in With Chris Hayes*, June 17, 2015

"I think if you look at the Irish booking odds right now, Jeb Bush is a 7–1 favorite to win the presidency, Marco Rubio is 7–2."

> —Hugh Hewitt, conservative radio host, MSNBC's *Up with Steve Kornacki*, June 20, 2015

CHRIS WALLACE, FOX NEWS: Let me ask you a couple of questions. How should Republicans handle Donald Trump?

KARL ROVE, REPUBLICAN STRATEGIST: Ignore him. Look, he is completely off the base.... This guy is not a serious candidate.

> —*Fox News Sunday*, June 21, 2015

"Jeb Bush, who might be president, and Donald Trump, who won't be president, competing for media oxygen, and well, it was a contest."

> —Howard Kurtz, host, Fox News' *MediaBuzz*, June 21, 2015

"Anyone who takes [Trump] seriously should really, really, really be ashamed."

> —Michelle Bernard, president of the Bernard Center for Women, MSNBC's *Hardball with Chris Matthews*, June 23, 2015

"At the end of the day, it's quite possible that Donald Trump will get 11 percent in New Hampshire, but that might be his cap."

—Patrick Murray, director of the Monmouth University Polling Institute, *Politico*, June 24, 2015

"If anything, Trump's current poll numbers suggest his weakness."

—Daniel W. Drezner, professor at the Fletcher School of Law and Diplomacy at Tufts University, *The Washington Post*, July 2, 2015

"Donald Trump will not be the Republican nominee. There's absolutely no way—his unfavorables are above 60 percent."

—Lisa Boothe, Republican strategist, CNN's *New Day*, July 4, 2015

"The early Republican polls showing Trump in second position behind Jeb Bush are hilarious—and meaningless."

—Carl Hiaasen, author and columnist, "There Will Never Be a President Trump," *The Miami Herald*, July 11, 2015

"Let's start with this: Donald Trump is not going to be the Republican presidential nominee in 2016."

—Chris Cillizza, *The Washington Post*, July 12, 2015

"I'm pretty confident that when we're waiting for the votes to be counted in Iowa and New Hampshire, we won't be talking about Donald Trump."

—Stuart Stevens, Mitt Romney's chief political strategist, MSNBC's *The Last Word with Lawrence O'Donnell*, July 13, 2015

"I do not believe we will be talking much about Donald Trump in November, December, [and] January."

> —Charles Cook, editor of *The Cook Political Report*, MSNBC's *The Last Word with Lawrence O'Donnell*, July 13, 2015

"I don't think Donald Trump is going to be the nominee of the Republican Party."

> —Rich Galen, Republican strategist, CNN's *Anderson Cooper 360°*, July 15, 2015

"Don Voyage! Trump Is Toast After Insult: 'McCain Not a War Hero'"

> —*New York Post* headline, July 19, 2015

"Trump's support will probably fade. Or at least, given his high unfavorable ratings, it will plateau, and other candidates will surpass him as the rest of the field consolidates."

> —Nate Silver, FiveThirtyEight, July 20, 2015

"There is no chance that Donald Trump is going to be nominated by the Republican Party as their presidential nominee."

> —Ryan Lizza, Washington correspondent for *The New Yorker*, CNN *Tonight*, July 20, 2015

"The Donald Trump candidacy is almost over. Don't be fooled by Trump's double-digit lead in a new poll: He is not going to win. . . . Donald Trump is not running a real campaign. . . . Soon, the bolder members of the field will follow Rick Perry, Marco Rubio, and Jeb Bush in making harder and more decisive strokes against him. Unlike Trump, they'll use real oppo, tested, and targeted messages—ads built not just to cut, but to kill. They'll break his operational tempo, get inside his OODA loop, and turn his circus into a crispy ruin. It's what real campaigns do."

> —Rick Wilson, Republican message and media strategist, *Politico*,
> July 22, 2015

"[Trump's] unfavorable ratings are extraordinarily high. So this is not a popular person. And people tend, in the end, to vote for people they like."

> —Gerald Seib, Washington bureau chief of *The Wall Street Journal*, CBS
> News' *Face the Nation*, July 26, 2015

"Donald Trump will not be the Republican nominee, in almost—almost all certainty."

> —John Heilemann, co-managing editor of Bloomberg Politics, CBS
> News' *Face the Nation*, July 26, 2015

"At the end of the day, [Trump] is not going to be the Republican nominee."

> —Sara Fagen, Republican strategist and former political director for
> President George W. Bush, NBC News' *Meet the Press*, July 26, 2015

"He hit a ceiling now, at 20 percent? When you look at his negatives in New Hampshire, he's got 53 percent. There's nowhere to go after 20 percent."

> —Amy Walter, national editor of *The Cook Political Report*, NBC News'
> *Meet the Press*, July 26, 2015

"I think Trump is not going to win the nomination."

—Ron Fournier, senior political columnist for *National Journal*, NBC
News' *Meet the Press*, July 26, 2015

"I run into very few people who think Donald Trump is likely to be the nominee of the Republican Party," (a feat accomplished by not inviting them to his program). "The second thing is that Donald Trump has a high floor relative to everybody else. He's got 20 percent. He's also got a low ceiling."

—Karl Rove, Republican strategist, *Fox News Sunday*, August 2, 2015

JOHN BRABENDER, REPUBLICAN POLITICAL CONSULTANT:
Donald Trump is not going to be the nominee. I'm telling you that right now. But . . .
DON LEMON, HOST: How do you say that?
BRABENDER: He's not just going to be. My experience of doing this for 30 years. I'm just telling you he's not going to be the nominee.

—*CNN Tonight*, August 3, 2015

"Donald Trump is doing well now, but I rather suspect the air will come out of that balloon at some point in time. I don't know when, I don't know how, but it's very difficult to imagine him being the Republican nominee for president."

—Larry Sabato, director of the Center for Politics at the University of
Virginia, CNN's *World Right Now with Hala Gorani*, August 5, 2015

"He's an entertainer. And therefore he's popular. But he will not be the nominee."

—Charlie Black, Republican political strategist, MSNBC's *Hardball with
Chris Matthews*, August 5, 2015

"Trump's campaign will fail by one means or another.... If you want absurd specificity, I recently estimated Trump's chance of becoming the GOP nominee at 2 percent."

—Nate Silver, FiveThirtyEight, August 6, 2015

"Let me go on the record saying this right now: Donald Trump will not be our next president. He won't even be the GOP nominee. And I know, I know: We've underestimated him before. But still."

—Amber Phillips, *The Washington Post*, August 10, 2015

"Our emphatic prediction is simply that Trump will not win the nomination. It's not even clear that he's trying to do so."

—Nate Silver, FiveThirtyEight, August 11, 2015

"Virtually all the political prognosticators are united on one point: Donald Trump's surge is fascinating, but of course he won't be the Republican nominee."

—Howard Kurtz, host Fox News' *MediaBuzz*, August 16, 2015

"Whomever is going to be the eventual nominee ... it's not going be Donald Trump."

—Robert George, editorial board member of *The New York Daily News*, MSNBC's *Up with Steve Kornacki*, August 16, 2015

"I do think that Trump will hit a ceiling.... So, at the end of the day, I don't believe that Trump will be the nominee."

—Mindy Finn, Republican political consultant, *CNN Newsroom*, August 18, 2015

"[Trump is] here to stay for a while, maybe through a few primaries. But he is not going be the nominee. . . . When the field narrows, he won't go very far."

> —Charlie Black, NBC News' *Meet the Press*, August 23, 2015

"Donald Trump, who is not going to be the nominee . . ."

> —Alex Castellanos, Republican presidential campaign veteran, NBC News' *Meet the Press*, August 23, 2015

"I'm going to show you Donald Trump will not be the nominee of the Republican Party!"

> —Adolfo Franco, Republican strategist, MSNBC's *Hardball with Chris Matthews*, August 28, 2015

"I am sure Donald Trump will not be our party nominee."

> —Adolfo Franco, MSNBC's *Up with Steve Kornacki*, August 30, 2015

"[It] won't happen, won't happen. I mean, Trump has . . . I think he's hit a ceiling of about 30 percent. . . . We're at peak Trump. Of course, I said this about six weeks ago. . . . Maybe peak Trump will last for another two, three weeks, but I don't think so . . . I do not believe [Trump] can be the nominee."

> —William Kristol, editor of *The Weekly Standard*, ABC's *This Week with George Stephanopoulos*, September 6, 2015

"Last week's debate . . . could mark the leveling off of Trump's rise and the beginning of his deflation."

> —Thomas Fitzgerald, politics writer, *The Philadelphia Inquirer*, September 20, 2015

"He is getting boring. That's what destroys Trump. . . . I will be stunned if the next time you and I sit down at this table he still has the numbers that he has now."

—Ian Bremmer, political scientist, PBS's *Charlie Rose*,
September 22, 2015

"The entire commentariat is going to feel a little silly when Marco Rubio wins every Republican primary."

—Ross Douthat, columnist for *The New York Times*, Twitter,
September 25, 2015

"Carson, Fiorina, and Trump are not going to be our nominee. It is a two-man race, Jeb versus Marco."

—A "senior GOP strategist," quoted in Chris Cillizza's column in *The
Washington Post*, September 29, 2015

"Ultimately, I don't think he'll ever put himself at the mercy of actual voters in a primary."

—Joe Nocera, columnist for *The New York Times*, "Is Donald Trump
Serious?", September 29, 2015

"You would see him spending a lot more money if he were putting together a true national infrastructure."

—Rick Wilson, quoted in Joe Nocera's "Is Donald Trump Serious?" *The
New York Times*, September 29, 2015

"I don't think [Trump's] going to be on the ballot by February 1."

—Stuart Stevens, CNN's *The Lead with Jake Tapper*, October 5, 2015

"It's true that Trump continues to maintain a comfortable lead in national polling—about 10 percentage points ahead of Ben Carson, and another 10 or more over the rest of the field. . . . Despite that, nothing so far tells us that Trump has any serious chance of being the Republican nominee."

—Jonathan Bernstein, columnist for *Bloomberg View*, "Seriously, Trump Won't Win," October 19, 2015

"And 26.2 percent, Mr. Trump's number in the RealClear-Politics average, is still a long way from 50 percent. . . . He actually peaked in the RealClearPolitics average, Mr. Trump did. . . . He peaked on September 19th, declined, and has risen a little recently."

—Karl Rove, Fox News, *On the Record with Greta Van Susteren*, October 20, 2015

"No major party has ever nominated a figure like Trump . . . and I don't believe that the 2016 G.O.P. will be the first."

—Ross Douthat, *The New York Times*, October 24, 2015

"Sen. Marco Rubio leads the Republican pack in Iowa—at least according to CNN's Political Prediction Market. . . . For the Republican nomination, the Prediction Market reveals that Rubio is leading that front, with his odds currently at 46%. Trump's chances for the nomination are at 22% and Cruz is at 12%."

—Daniella Diaz, digital producer for CNN Politics, November 19, 2015

"Nobody remotely like Trump has won a major-party nomination in the modern era. . . . That adds up to Trump's chances being higher than 0 but (considerably) less than 20 percent."

—Nate Silver, FiveThirtyEight, November 23, 2015

"Do I think it's likely [that Trump will win the nomination]?
No.... There are candidates who can plausibly win the nom-
ination.... If I'm betting money—three: Bush, Christie,
Rubio."

—Karl Rove, MSNBC's *Morning Joe*, November 25, 2015

STEVE INSKEEP, HOST: Well, what's happening now in the
Republican Party?
KARL ROVE: They're a group of people who are so angry....
Look, I'm going to be for the Republican nominee, whoever
that is. But I do think that politicians who are successful
are people who add, don't subtract.

—*Morning Edition*, NPR, December 3, 2015

"Facing an existential electoral threat in the form of Donald
Trump's nomination, the rest of the party will unite around
a candidate. Right now, I think Ted Cruz is very likely to be
that guy."

—Chris Stirewalt, Fox Business' *Lou Dobbs Tonight*, December 8, 2015

"Where's Donald Trump going to win? Iowa? Don't think so....
Fourth is where I think he'll end up in Iowa.... I'd say the top
three in New Hampshire will be Christie, Rubio, and Bush."

—Stuart Stevens, quoted in Chris Cillizza's "Mitt Romney's top
strategist thinks Donald Trump won't win a thing," *The Washington
Post*, December 11, 2015

"In the Monmouth poll, which is well regarded, if you look at
their data on repeat likely [Iowa] caucus-goers, Trump is fourth."

—George Will, *Fox News Sunday*, December 13, 2015

"What does a brokered convention mean? What it means is that nobody arrives in Cleveland with a majority of the delegates. That's likely to happen . . ."

> —Karl Rove, *Fox News Sunday*, December 13, 2015

"Donald Trump will not be the Republican nominee."

> —John Harwood, CNBC's Washington correspondent,
> December 31, 2015

"I'll be surprised if it is a choice between Donald Trump and Bernie Sanders, and I would bet against both of them to be party nominees."

> —Larry Sabato, *CNN Newsroom*, January 18, 2016

"Trump cannot get 51% in a head-to-head against any Republican candidate remaining in the race."

> —Bradley Todd, veteran Republican political strategist, quoted in
> Adam Edelman's "Donald Trump, Despite N.H. Primary Victory,
> Faces Tough Task to Win GOP Nomination," *New York Daily News*,
> February 11, 2016

"I really do believe last night could be a moment where finally Republican voters say enough. . . . And finally, maybe people will focus on: Can and should he be president of the United States? And I think Republican primary voters will say no."

> —William Kristol, ABC's *This Week with George Stephanopoulos*,
> February 14, 2016

"There are lots of scenarios by which Trump could be denied the nomination."

> —Larry Sabato, *CNN Newsroom*, February 21, 2016

"But what if Donald Trump already is stopped? What if he's stopped in the mid-thirties? . . . Rubio wins some of these other states, goes into Florida and wins that—what if there's a Romney endorsement? . . . Rubio may have won the nomination."

> —Alex Castellanos, ABC's *This Week with George Stephanopoulos,*
> **February 21, 2016**

"I don't believe Donald Trump is ultimately going to be the nominee. It may . . . come down to a bloody fight on the convention floor, but I don't believe ultimately he will represent the party in November."

> —Sara Fagen, ABC's *This Week with George Stephanopoulos,*
> **February 21, 2016**

"I believe Marco Rubio is going to win Florida. . . . And I think a month from now, we may be back here talking about an open convention, because I think old rules apply."

> —Hugh Hewitt, conservative radio host, NBC's *Meet the Press,*
> **February 21, 2016**

"But I also think it's probable [Trump] will not have 50 percent of the delegates. . . . So we could go for the first time since 1948 to a second ballot or even a third ballot, where I can assure you that Trump will not be the nominee."

> —Michael Medved, conservative radio host, MSNBC's *The Rachel Maddow Show,* **February 24, 2016**

"I think ultimately Marco Rubio is going to be the nominee this fall."

> —Jason Roe, senior adviser to Marco Rubio, *CNN Newsroom,*
> **February 24, 2016**

"And whoever beats Donald Trump will have the right to be the nominee."

—Stuart Stevens, CNN's *Anderson Cooper 360°*, March 4, 2016

"Donald Trump would literally have to win every—half the delegates remaining between now and the end of this—to be the nominee. And he's not on pace to do that."

—Senator Marco Rubio, CNN's *Early Start*, March 8, 2016

"If Ohio and Florida split, I think there's a pretty good chance to stop Trump. I agree, people are being much too fatalistic. "

—William Kristol, ABC's *This Week with George Stephanopoulos*,
March 13, 2016

"I still believe that Donald Trump will not be the nominee."

—Sen. Marco Rubio, ABC's *This Week with George Stephanopoulos*,
March 13, 2016

"Trump's probability of winning the nomination fell to 44 percent on Friday from 67 percent a week ago. . . . The probability that the Republicans will have a brokered convention to decide the nominee for the Nov. 8 election jumped to 69 percent from 43 percent a week ago, according to PredictIt, an online predictions market where users place money on who they think will win the election."

—Anjali Athavaley, Reuters, April 1, 2016

"[Trump] is probably not going to be the Republican nominee after all."

—Jacob Weisberg, *Slate*, April 8, 2016

"Republican insiders overwhelmingly believe this summer's national convention will require multiple ballots to select the presidential nominee."

—Steven Shepard, campaigns editor for *Politico*, "Insiders: 90 Percent Predict Contested GOP Convention," *Politico*, April 8, 2016

•   •   •

The Drudge Report, April 28, 2016: Trump most votes in Republican history.

Notes

1. CNN Live Event/Special: Saddleback Presidential Candidates Forum, August 17, 2008.
2. CNN Live Event/Special: Democratic Debate in Las Vegas, November 17, 2007.
3. "Mayor Antonio Villaraigosa, D–Los Angeles, Delivers Remarks at the National Press Club on Immigration Reform," *Political Transcript Wire*, January 15, 2013.
4. Biana Barragan, "More Than Half of Los Angeles Speaks a Language Other Than English at Home, *Curbed LA*, November 4, 2015, available at http://la.curbed.com/2015/11/4/9904020/los-angeles-languages.
5. Ron Unz, "California Republicans Vote to Restore 'Bilingual Education,'" *Unz Review*, May 7, 2014, available at http://www.unz2016.org/article/california-republicans-vote-to-restore-bilingual-education.
6. Mark Tushnet, "Abandoning Defensive Crouch Liberal Constitutionalism," *Balkinization* blog, May 6, 2016, available at http://balkin.blogspot.it/2016/05/abandoning-defensive-crouch-liberal.html?m=1.
7. Michael C. Moynihan, Twitter post, May 3, 2016, https://twitter.com/mcmoynihan/status/727639668641153024.
8. Stephen Collinson and Maeve Reston, "Donald Trump's Next Reality Show: 2016," CNN.com, June 17, 2015.
9. Katherine Faulders, "Rand Paul Says GOP Must Get 'Beyond Deportation,'" ABC News, April 1, 2014, available at http://abcnews.go.com/blogs/politics/2014/04/rand-paul-says-gop-must-get-beyond-deportation.
10. Ed O'Keefe, "In a New Appeal to Hispanics, Jeb Bush Deploys His 'Secret Weapon'—Columba Bush," *Washington Post*, September 14, 2015, available at https://www.washingtonpost.com/news/post-politics/wp/2015/09/14/in-a-new-appeal-to-hispanics-jeb-bush-deploys-his-secret-weapon-columba-bush.

11. *Meet the Press*, NBC, September 20, 2015.

12. Hillary Rodham Clinton, *Living History* (New York: Simon & Schuster, 2003).

13. "Donald Trump, Republican Presidential Candidate, Delivers Remarks at the Family Leadership Summit," *Political Transcript Wire*, July 20, 2015.

14. "A Note About Our Coverage of Donald Trump's 'Campaign,'" *Huffington Post*, July 7, 2015.

15. Neil Irwin, "Quantitative Easing Is Ending. Here's What It Did, in Charts," *New York Times*, October 29, 2014.

16. Fox News Sunday, Fox News, July 19, 2015; *CBS This Morning*, CBS, November 23, 2015; *The O'Reilly Factor*, Fox News, January 14, 2016; *The Five*, Fox News, January 14, 2016; *The Five*, Fox News, January 25, 2016; *The Five*, Fox News, January 27, 2016; *The Kelly File*, Fox News, March 21, 2016; *Your World with Neil Cavuto*, Fox News, April 18, 2016; *Fox News Sunday*, Fox News, May 29, 2016.

17. See Gregory Wallace, "The Anti-Trump Movement Spent Upwards of $75 Million and Ultimately Lost," CNN, May 4, 2016, available at http://cnn.com/2016/05/04/politics/anti-donald-trump-movement-75-million-lost.

18. Chrystia Freeland, "The Rise of the New Global Elite," *The Atlantic*, January 2011, available at http://www.theatlantic.com/magazine/archive/2011/01/the-rise-of-the-new-global-elite/308343.

19. Nicholas Ballasy, "Albright: Flyover Country Shows There's Room for More Refugees," PJ Media, September 23, 2015, available at https://pjmedia.com/blog/albright-flyover-country-shows-theres-room-for-more-refugees.

20. Julie McMahon, "Madeleine Albright Calls for Bipartisan Compromise, U.S. Acceptance of Refugees in Talk at SU," *The Syracuse Post-Standard*, April 5, 2016, available at http://www.syracuse.com/su-news/index.ssf/2016/04/madeleine_albright_calls_for_b.html.

21. Stephen Battaglio, "Local TV Stations Counting on Political Ads Worry About Donald Trump's Ability to Get Free Airtime," *Los Angeles Times*, April 14, 2016, available at http://www.latimes.com/entertainment/envelope/cotown/la-et-0414-ct-trump-ad-spending-20160414-story.html.

22. Sports programming advertising, accounting for nearly 40 percent of all TV revenue, brought in $8.47 billion for ABC, CBS, NBC, and Fox in 2014–15. Anthony Crupi, "Sports Now Accounts for 37% of Broadcast TV Ad Spending," *Advertising Age*, September 10, 2015, available at http://adage.com/article/media/sports-account-37-percent-all-tv-ad-dollars/300310.

23. Eric Lichtblau and Nicholas Confessore, "Reports Detail Shift in Finance of Campaigns," *New York Times*, July 16, 2015.

24. Matea Gold and Anu Narayanswamy, "GOP Haul Shows a Pivot to Groups Backed by Rich Elite," *Washington Post*, July 16, 2015.

25. Ibid.

26. Dan Balz, "Trump 2016: Summer Rerun or a Headache-Inducing New Series for GOP?" *Washington Post,* July 12, 2015.

27. Jeb Bush's Facebook page, https://www.facebook.com/jebbush.

28. Stephen Battaglio, "The Biz: The Research Memo That Almost Killed *Seinfeld*," *TV Guide,* June 27, 2014, available at http://www.tvguide.com/news/seinfeld-research-memo-1083639.

29. *CNN Newsroom,* January 30, 2016.

30. See Kelley Vlahos, "The Shifting Military Vote," *The American Conservative,* November 4, 2008, available at http://www.theamericanconservative.com/2008/11/04/the-shifting-military-vote.

31. Alan Abramowitz and Ruy Teixeira, "The Decline of the White Working Class and Other Changes in the Class Structure," Brookings Institution, February 28, 2008, available at http://www.brookings.edu/~/media/Events/2008/2/28-america/0228_america_teixeira2ppt.PDF.

32. Tessa Berenson, "How Ted Cruz Is Using Spanish in His Presidential Campaign," *Time,* March 23, 2015, available at http://time.com/3754151/ted-cruz-spanish-campaign.

33. "Monty Python—Four Yorkshiremen," YouTube, posted June 20, 2006, https://www.youtube.com/watch?v=Xe1a1wHxTyo.

34. *World News Tonight,* ABC, September 2, 1986; "Intervention by Trump Helps Stave Off Foreclosure of Family Farm," Associated Press, September 3, 1986; Jerry Schwartz, "Widow, Her Farm Saved, Burns the Mortgage," Associated Press December 23, 1986.

35. "GOP Presidential Debate in Las Vegas," CNN, December 15, 2015.

36. ABC News and *The Independent Journal Review*: Republican Presidential Candidates Debate, February 7, 2016.

37. Steven V. Roberts, "Nonvoters Played Key Role in Election," *New York Times,* November 5, 1980.

38. See, e.g., George H. W. Bush "Family/Children" 1988 ad campaign, posted December 26, 2009, available at https://www.youtube.com/watch?v=LToAmI4r6ms.

39. Tom Fiedler, "Askew in '84 Spotlights Shift in Democratic Party," *Miami Herald,* January 12, 1992.

40. "Ted Cruz—Mobilizing Christians to 'Vote Biblical Values' Is the Key to Saving America," RWW News, August 11, 2015, available at https://www.youtube.com/watch?v=oAeiZCAmBf8.

41. Richard Danker memo, quoted in William Kristol, "What Trump Saw and Cruz Did Not," *The Weekly Standard,* April 26, 2016, available at http://www.weeklystandard.com/what-trump-saw-and-cruz-did-not/article/2002126.

42. "After the Attacks: Reaction from Around the World," *New York Times,* September 13, 2001.

43. *Fox Special Report with Bret Baier,* Fox News Network, July 6, 2015.

44. *Fox Special Report with Bret Baier,* Fox News Network, June 16, 2015.

45. ABC News and *The Independent Journal Review:* Republican Presidential Candidates Debate, February 7, 2016.

46. Stephen Battaglio, "Fox News' Bret Baier Boosts Profile with Well-Prepared, 'Offramp'-Blocking Showing as a GOP Debate Moderator," *Los Angeles Times,* August 10, 2015.

47. Ryan Lizza, Twitter post, June 17, 2013, https://twitter.com/RyanLizza/status/346736094932504576/photo/1. ("Since there seems to be interest in Rubio aide's quote that appeared in my piece, here's some more context" [interview transcript].)

48. In a nutshell, Reagan shocked the entire foreign policy community by taking an all-new approach to the threat of nuclear annihilation during the Cold War. Instead of détente, mutual assured destruction, or "co-existence," he said we were at war and we should win. (See Ann Coulter, *Treason: Liberal Treachery from the Cold War to the War on Terrorism,* chap. 8.) Hysteria ensued. Instead of continuing to try to squeeze blood from a turnip on taxes, Reagan said he'd slash taxes and bring in more revenue to the federal government. Hysteria ensued. Reagan did both, destroyed the Soviet empire, and brought in more revenue with massive tax cuts. See every third column ever written by Thomas Sowell.

49. "Editorial: The Reagan Theory," *New York Times,* October 6, 1980; "Editorial: Mr. Reagan's Missile Gap," *New York Times,* October 7, 1980.

50. Fox Business Network, 2016 Republican Presidential Candidates Debate, November 11, 2015.

51. ABC News and *The Independent Journal Review:* Republican Presidential Candidates Debate, February 7, 2016.

52. CNN: Republican Debate, September 16, 2015.

53. ABC News and *The Independent Journal Review:* Republican Presidential Candidates Debate, February 7, 2016.

54. Fox Business Network Republican Presidential Debate, January 29, 2016.

55. ABC News and *The Independent Journal Review:* Republican Presidential Candidates Debate, February 7, 2016.

56. Ibid.

57. MSNBC Special: GOP Presidential Debate, September 7, 2011.

58. Fox News, Republican Presidential Candidates Debate, August 11, 2011.

59. CNN: Republican Debate, September 16, 2015.

60. "Well, first of all, I have an understanding of exactly what it is Russia and Putin are doing, and it's pretty straightforward. He wants to reposition Russia, once again, as a geopolitical force . . . [zzzzzzzzzz] . . . What [Putin] is doing is he is trying to replace us as the single most important power broker in the Middle East, and this president is allowing it. That is what

is happening in the Middle East. That's what's happening with Russia, and . . ." [*Buzzer*]. CNN: Republican Debate, September 16, 2015.

61. CNN: Republican Presidential Debate, December 15, 2015.

62. CNN: Republican Debate, September 16, 2015.

63. "What's important to do is we must deal frontally with this threat of radical Islamists, especially from ISIS. . . . We also understand that this is a group that's growing in its governance of territory. It's not just Iraq and Syria. They are now a predominant group in Libya. They are beginning to pop up in Afghanistan. They are increasingly involved now in attacks in Yemen. They have Jordan in their sights. This group needs to be confronted with serious proposals." CNN, Republican Presidential Debate, December 15, 2015.

64. See, e.g., Mark Muro and Siddharth Kulkarn, "Voter Anger Explained—in One Chart," Brookings, March 15, 2016, available at http://www.brook ings.edu/blogs/the-avenue/posts/2016/03/15-voter-anger-explained-muro -kulkarni; Adam Robinson, "American Manufacturing Jobs Not Going to Return to Previous Levels . . . and That's OK" (Motley Fool chart), Cerasis .com, August 11, 2014, available at http://cerasis.com/2014/08/11/american -manufacturing-jobs.

65. Ross Douthat, "The Conservative Case Against Trump," *New York Times,* May 7, 2016.

66. Glenn Kessler, "President Obama and the 'Red Line' on Syria's Chemical Weapons," *Washington Post,* September 6, 2013.

67. Russell Goldman, "John McCain Border Shift: 'Complete Danged Fence,'" ABC News, May 11, 2010, available at http://abcnews.go.com/Politics/ john-mccain-immigration-reversal-complete-danged-fence/story?id= 10616090.

68. Amy Sherman, "Hillary Clinton's Changing Position on Same-Sex Marriage," PolitiFact, June 17, 2015, available at http://www.politifact .com/truth-o-meter/statements/2015/jun/17/hillary-clinton/hillary-clinton -change-position-same-sex-marriage.

69. Ibid.

70. *This Week,* ABC, August 16, 2015.

71. *Journal Editorial Report,* Fox News Network, January 24, 2016.

72. Doug Heye, "As a Republican Operative, Here's Why I Won't Support Trump If He Is the Nominee," *Independent Journal Opinion,* January 25, 2016, available at http://opinion.injo.com/2016/01/251811-as-a-republican -operative-heres-why-i-wont-support-trump-if-he-is-the-nominee.

73. Federal law states: "Suspension of entry or imposition of restrictions by President. Whenever the President finds that the entry of any aliens or of any class of aliens into the United States would be detrimental to the interests of the United States, he may by proclamation, and for such period as he shall deem necessary, suspend the entry of all aliens or any class of

aliens as immigrants or nonimmigrants, or impose on the entry of aliens any restrictions he may deem to be appropriate." Immigration and Nationality Act, 8 U.S.C. 1182.

74. Mark Hensch, "Clinton Ally: Trump's 'Schlonged' Remark Implies Obama's 'a Black Rapist,'" *The Hill,* December 23, 2015, available at http://thehill.com/blogs/ballot-box/presidential-races/264108-clinton-ally-schlonged-implies-obamas-a-black-rapist.

75. *All In with Chris Hayes,* MSNBC, May 26, 2016.

76. *Meet the Press,* NBC, February 28, 2016.

77. *The Kelly File,* Fox News Network, February 26, 2016.

78. Ibid.

79. "Trump and the Protesters," *Wall Street Journal,* March 14, 2016.

80. See, e.g., "Looting, Fatal Stabbing Follow in Wake of N.Y. Racial Melee," *Chicago Tribune,* August 21, 1991 ("Activist Minister Rev. Al Sharpton was greeted by a loud cheer when he arrived at about 6:45 p.m. and went to the apartment where one of the two injured cousins lived. Demanding the arrest of the driver, Sharpton denounced what he called 'an apartheid ambulance service' and warned: 'We are on the verge of an explosion.' Groups of black youths then rampaged through Crown Heights, [Police Commissioner Lee] Brown said. Shortly before midnight, a 29-year-old Hasidic student was fatally stabbed, apparently in retaliation for the black boy's death, Brown said."); and "3 Charged, 4 Still Sought in Breslin Assault," *New York Times,* August 29, 1991, available at http://www.nytimes.com/1991/08/29/nyregion/3-charged-4-still-sought-in-breslin-assault.html ("Three youths, including an 11-year-old boy, have been arrested on charges of assaulting and robbing the columnist Jimmy Breslin as he was covering the Crown Heights disturbances in Brooklyn, the police said yesterday. Mr. Breslin, who writes for *New York Newsday,* was assaulted on Aug. 21 by a crowd of youths, who forced him from a taxi cab, beat him up, stripped him to his underwear and robbed him, the police said."); Ronald Sullivan, "3 Youths Guilty of Rape And Assault of Jogger," *New York Times,* August 19, 1990 ("Throughout the trial the Manhattan courthouse at 111 Centre Street has been the scene of frequent and volatile demonstrations, most by people protesting that the trial was grounded in racism.... Last night a leader of the protest, the Rev. Al Sharpton, said the convictions 'will inflame the city.'"); "Trial Sets Alight a Bonfire of Profanities," *Courier-Mail* (UK), August 1, 1990 ("Earlier, similar violence had been directed at television cameramen and reporters . . ."); Barbara Goldberg, "Decision to Hold Youths Convicted in Jogger Case Criticized," United Press International, August 19, 1990 ("McCray's father, Bobby McCray, Sunday knocked down television and radio equipment outside his Harlem apartment building as reporters gathered for a news conference by the Rev. Al Sharpton, who has been a family adviser."); Catherine

Crocker, "Jogger Case Touches Raw Nerve in New York City," Associated Press, August 20, 1990 ("During the trial, tensions ran high outside the courthouse. . . . News photographers were punched by supporters of the defendants.")

81. *Today,* NBC, March 11, 2016.

82. "Editorial: Stopping Arizona," *New York Times,* April 30, 2010.

83. Linda Greenhouse, "Breathing While Undocumented," *New York Times,* April 27, 2010.

84. Dana Milbank, "Obama's Fatal Flinch on Immigration," *Washington Post,* May 2, 2010.

85. "Top 10 Dumbest Things Said About the Arizona Immigration Law," *San Francisco Examiner,* April 30, 2010, available at http://www.sfexaminer .com/top-10-dumbest-things-said-about-the-arizona-immigration-law.

86. Ibid.

87. Andy Barr, "Republicans Hit Arizona Law," *Politico,* April 28, 2010.

88. "Top 10 Dumbest Things Said About the Arizona Immigration Law," *San Francisco Examiner,* May 19, 2016.

89. *The Ed Show,* MSNBC, April 28, 2010.

90. M. J. Lee and Pat St. Claire, "Trump Draws Thousands in Phoenix, Continues Immigration Theme," CNN Wire, July 12, 2015.

91. Ryan Lizza, "John McCain Has a Few Things to Say About Donald Trump," *The New Yorker,* July 16, 2015.

92. "Donald Trump, Republican Presidential Candidate, Delivers Remarks at the Family Leadership Summit," *Political Transcript Wire,* July 20, 2015.

93. Kathy Frankovic, "Donald Trump's Support Remains High Following John McCain Controversy," YouGov, July 24, 2015, available at https:// today.yougov.com/news/2015/07/24/trumps-support-remains-high-mccain -controversy.

94. *Fox News Sunday,* Fox News Network, July 19, 2015.

95. Serge F. Kovaleski and Fredrick Kunkle, "Northern New Jersey Draws Probers' Eyes," *Washington Post,* September 18, 2001, available at https:// www.washingtonpost.com/archive/politics/2001/09/18/northern-new-jer sey-draws-probers-eyes/40f82ea4-e015-4d6e-a87e-93aa433fafdc.

96. "Jersey City 9/11 Celebration Report CBS," YouTube, posted December 1, 2015, available at https://www.youtube.com/watch?v=3auKMH kZJnQ.

97. Kevin Fagan, "Muslim Enclave Under Strain of Terror Backlash," *San Francisco Chronicle,* September 22, 2001.

98. Julianne Ross, "Trump Is Wrong About People 'Cheering' 9/11 in New Jersey—We Dug Up the Video That Proves It," MTV.com, November 25, 2015, available at http://www.mtv.com/news/2549792/donald-trump -new-jersey-muslim-comments.

99. "4 Howard Stern Callers Confirms Trump: Muslims Did Cheer After 9/11," YouTube, posted December 1, 2015, available at https://www.youtube.com/watch?v=1ErS12XaSDE.

100. Fred Siegel, "The Problem Is Radical Islam," *New York Post,* September 14, 2001.

101. Amy Wilentz, "The Way We Live Now: 9-30-01: Close Reading: Elements of War; The Suspect," *New York Times,* September 30, 2001.

102. Serge F. Kovaleski and Fredrick Kunkle, "Northern New Jersey Draws Probers' Eyes," *Washington Post,* September 18, 2001.

103. "Editorial: The War Against America; The National Defense," *New York Times,* September 12, 2001.

104. "Arabs and Muslims Steer Through an Unsettling Scrutiny," *New York Times,* September 13, 2001; "For Arab-Americans, Flag-Flying and Fear," *New York Times,* September 14, 2001; Laurie Goodstein and Gustav Niebuhr, "Attacks and Harassment of Arab-Americans Increase," *New York Times,* September 14, 2001.

105. *New Day,* CNN, December 1, 2015.

106. Mark Mueller, "Exclusive: Some Jersey City Muslims Did Celebrate 9/11, Cop and Residents Say," NJ Advance Media, December 21, 2015, available at http://www.nj.com/news/index.ssf/2015/12/exclusive_jersey_city_cop_residents_say_some_musli.html.

107. Ibid.

108. Ibid.

109. Ibid.

110. Ibid.

111. Ross, "Trump Is Wrong About People 'Cheering'" (see note 106).

112. Tommy Christopher, "Rudy Giuliani 'Confirms' 9/11 Celebrations in Unbelievable Way," *Mediaite,* December 1, 2015, available at http://www.mediaite.com/tv/rudy-giuliani-confirms-911-celebrations-in-unbelievable-way.

113. Lauren Carroll, "New Information Doesn't Fix Donald Trump's 9/11 Claim," PolitiFact, December 2, 2015, available at http://www.politifact.com/truth-o-meter/article/2015/dec/02/new-information-doesnt-fix-donald-trumps-911-claim.

114. Glenn Kessler, "Trump's Outrageous Claim That 'Thousands' of New Jersey Muslims Celebrated the 9/11 Attacks," *Washington Post,* November 22, 2015.

115. Frank Wolfe, "Others Don't Recall What Clinton Does," *Arkansas Democrat-Gazette,* June 9, 1996.

116. Michael Fumento, "A Church Arson Epidemic? It's Smoke and Mirrors," *Wall Street Journal,* July 8, 1996; Michael Fumento, "Politics and Church Burnings," *Commentary,* October 1996; Michael Fumento, "USA Today's Arson Artistry," *American Spectator,* December 1996.

117. "Clinton's Speech Accepting the Democratic Nomination for President," *New York Times,* August 30, 1996.

118. "Army OKs Discharge of Soldier Accused of Painting Swastikas," *Patriot Ledger* (Quincy, Mass.), December 18, 1996.

119. Stelter told viewers that he had just spoken with Serge Kovaleski about his story, and "Serge says he spent days in Jersey City and he walked those streets and he tried to find any evidence that there were all these people celebrating. He found no evidence. He said to me—quote—'That was not the case, as best I can remember.'" *CNN Newsroom,* CNN, November 23, 2015.

120. "US Funds Restoration of Global Islamic Sites," Associated Press, August 24, 2010.

121. *CBS Evening News,* May 3, 2010.

122. *American Morning,* CNN, May 3, 2010.

123. Chuck Ross, "New Documents Prove Hillary Told Conflicting Stories About Video Blamed for Benghazi Attacks," *Daily Caller,* April 14, 2016, available at http://dailycaller.com/2016/04/14/new-documents-prove-hillary-told -conflicting-stories-about-benghazi-video/#ixzz4CSCmthNc.

124. *Fox News Sunday Roundtable,* Fox News Network, April 21, 2013.

125. Josh Gerstein, "Lynch Warns Against Anti-Muslim Backlash," *Politico,* December 3, 2015, available at http://www.politico.com/blogs/under-the-radar/2015/12/lynch-warns-against-anti-muslim-backlash-216421; Dan Riehl, "Loretta Lynch Vows to Prosecute Anti-Muslim Speech, Calls San Bernardino 'Wonderful Opportunity,'" Breitbart, December 4, 2015, available at http://www.breitbart.com/big-government/2015/12/04/ loretta-lynch-vows-prosecute-anti-muslim-speech-calls-san-bernardino -wonderful-opportunity.

126. Ian Schwartz, "NBC Terror Analyst: Gay Nightclub Shooting Possibly Was 'Domestic Terror' from 'White Hate Groups,'" RealClearPolitics, June 12, 2016, available at http://www.realclearpolitics.com/video/2016/06/12 /nbc_terror_analyst_gay_nightclub_shooting_possibly_was_domestic_ter ror_from_white_hate_groups.html.

127. "Investigators Look for Link Between Middle East Terrorists and Bombing in Oklahoma City," *CBS Evening News,* April 19, 1995. ("This was done with the attempt to inflict as many casualties as possible. That is a Middle Eastern trait and something that has been, generally, not carried out on this soil until we were rudely awakened to it in 1993.")

128. *The Last Word with Lawrence O'Donnell,* MSNBC, December 2, 2015. According to Nexis, only Fox News came right out and said the shooters were "Islamic motivated," in the excellent reporting of Aaron Cohen and Jim Hanson, with periodic interruptions from Bill O'Reilly warning them to be "very, very careful," and not to "speculate." *The O'Reilly Factor,* Fox News Network, December 2, 2015.

129. One month later, the *Los Angeles Times* admitted as much, deep in the middle of an article: "Farook spent about two hours at the center the

morning of the shooting, Bowdich said, socializing with coworkers gathered for a holiday event. Authorities haven't found any evidence to support suggestions that a workplace dispute led to the shooting, Bowdich said, adding that Farook's demeanor was normal that morning and that photos taken of him inside the facility during the event didn't show anything out of the ordinary." James Queally, Marisa Gerber, and Richard Winton, "Shooters' 18-Minute Gap Puzzles Investigators," *Los Angeles Times,* January 6, 2016.

130. *All In with Chris Hayes,* MSNBC, December 2, 2015.

131. Christopher Goffard, "Times Wins Pulitzer for San Bernardino Coverage," *Los Angeles Times,* April 19, 2016.

132. Joel Achenbach, "Terrorism? Workplace Violence? The Search for a Motive in San Bernardino," *Washington Post,* December 3, 2015, available at https://www.washingtonpost.com/news/post-nation/wp/2015/12/03/terrorism-workplace-violence-the-search-for-a-motive-in-san-bernardino.

133. Ibid.

134. Jim Yardley, Katrin Bennhold, Michael S. Schmidt, and Adam Nossiter, "Mounting Clues Point to Brothers and Trip to Syria," *New York Times,* November 16, 2015.

135. Editorial, "What Will Come After Paris?" *New York Times,* November 16, 2015.

136. "Officials Begin Putting Shooting Pieces Together," *Morning Edition,* NPR, November 6, 2009.

137. "For Muslims, Military Service Sometimes Met with Hostility," NPR, Part II, November 9, 2009, available at http://www.npr.org/templates/story/story.php?storyId=120238956. The chaplain, James Lee, also said his "immediate reaction" to the massacre at Fort Hood was to worry about the "immediate backlash again against the American-Muslim community here in the United States."

138. Foxnews.com "RAW DATA: Partial Transcript of Radical Cleric's Tape," March 18, 2010, available at http://www.foxnews.com/politics/2010/03/18/raw-data-partial-transcript-radical-clerics-tape.html; Lisa Daftari, "Al Qaeda to jihadis: 'Target white Americans, avoid minorities, because US mislabels attacks as 'hate crime,' "The Foreign Desk, June 24, 2016, available at http://www.foreigndesknews.com/world/us/al-qaeda-jihadis-target-white-americans-avoid-minorities-us-mislabels-attacks-hate-crime/.

139. Karen Attiah, "Charleston, Dylann Roof and the Racism of Millennials," *PostPartisan* blog, *Washington Post,* June 18, 2015.

140. Lydia Polgreen, "From Ferguson to Charleston, Anguish About Race Keeps Building," *New York Times,* June 21, 2015

141. Tim King, "Taliban Play Soccer with Decapitated Human Heads," Salem-News.com, December 28, 2013, available at http://www.salem-news.com/articles/december282013/taliban-beheaded-tk.php.

142. *All In with Chris Hayes,* MSNBC, December 8, 2015.

143. *The Rachel Maddow Show,* MSNBC, December 8, 2015.

144. "Muslim Americans: No Signs of Growth in Alienation or Support for Extremism," section 1: "A Demographic Portrait of Muslim Americans," Pew Research Center, August 30, 2011, available at http://www.people-press.org/2011/08/30/section-1-a-demographic-portrait-of-muslim-americans.

145. *Fox Special Report with Bret Baier,* Fox News Network, December 8, 2015.

146. *The Five,* Fox News Network, December 8, 2015.

147. Jennifer Agiesta, "Poll: 3-in-4 Say Benghazi Panel Politically Motivated," CNN, October 22, 2015, available at http://www.cnn.com/2015/10/22/politics/benghazi-committee-hillary-clinton-poll.

148. *Andrea Mitchell Reports,* MSNBC, December 8, 2015.

149. Peter Baker and Eric Schmitt, "Rampage Has U.S. Rethinking How to Stop Attacks," *New York Times,* December 6, 2015.

150. "The Trump Plans, If Ever Enacted, Could Come with Unintended Consequences," *NBC Nightly News,* December 8, 2015.

151. "Trump Defies Outrage," *CNN Newsroom,* December 8, 2015.

152. See, e.g., *The Rachel Maddow Show,* MSNBC, December 8, 2015; "Editorial: Trump's Dark Fantasy," *Chicago Tribune,* December 9, 2015.

153. See, e.g., Byron York, "In State After State, Strong GOP Support for Trump's Muslim Proposal," *The Examiner,* April 27, 2016; "Most Republicans Who Voted on Super Tuesday II Seek US Muslim Ban," *Sputnik News,* March 16, 2016, available at http://sputniknews.com/us/20160316/1036426397/majority-republicans-support-muslim-ban.html. Even Wisconsin! See ABC News Analysis Desk, Republican Primary Exit Poll Analysis, April 5, 2016, available at http://abcnews.go.com/Politics/live-republican-primary-exit-poll-analysis/story?id=38164180.

154. "Dangerous" (Sen. Lindsey Graham and Carly Fiorina); "scapegoating" (2012 GOP presidential nominee Mitt Romney); akin to "Hitler" (Former New Jersey Republican governor Christine Todd Whitman); "whiff of fascism" (GOP consultant Rick Wilson); and "absurd" (Fox News' Charles Krauthammer). See Tom McCarthy, Ben Jacobs, et al., "Donald Trump's Muslim Ban Plan Plunges Republican Party into Chaos," *The Guardian,* December 9, 2015, available at http://www.theguardian.com/us-news/2015/dec/08/donald-trump-muslim-ban-republican-party-chaos; Tom LoBianco, "Christine Todd Whitman: Donald Trump Muslim Comments Like Hitler's," CNN.com, December 9, 2015, available at http://www.cnn.com/2015/12/09/politics/christine-todd-whitman-donald-trump-hitler; "Donald Trump's Muslim US Ban Call Roundly Condemned," BBC News, December 8, 2015, available at http://www.bbc.com/news/world-us-canada-35037701; Byron York, "In State After State, Strong GOP Support for Trump's Muslim Proposal," *The Examiner,* April 27, 2016.

155. Haeyoun Park and Larry Buchanan, "Why It Takes Two Years for Syrian Refugees to Enter the U.S.," *New York Times,* November 20, 2015.

156. "USCIS Official Admits: No Syrian Database We Can Check," YouTube, posted October 5, 2015, available at https://www.youtube.com/watch?v= rQVz6seERZI.

157. "Syria; Communications," *The World Factbook,* Central Intelligence Agency, available at https://www.cia.gov/library/publications/the-world -factbook/geos/sy.html.

158. Scott Shane and Michael S. Schmidt, "Russia's Warning on Bombings Suspect Sets Off a Debate," *New York Times,* April 25, 2013.

159. *Special Report with Bret Baier,* Fox News Network, November 17, 2015.

160. *U.S. v. Waad Ramadan Alwan,* sentencing memorandum, January, 16, 2013, available at http://www.investigativeproject.org/documents/case_docs/ 2113.df; *U.S. v. Mohanad Shareef Hammadi,* arrest warrant, May 24, 2011, available at http://www.investigativeproject.org/documents/case_docs/1569.pdf.

161. Rebecca Boone, "Trial of Uzbek Man Opens in Boise," *Lewiston Morning Tribune,* July 15, 2015.

162. Katie Terhune, "Kurbanov Testifies in Boise Terrorism Trial," KTVB, July 31, 2015.

163. David Filipov, "Father of Man Killed by FBI Agents in Orlando, Fla., Says His Son Was Not Capable of Attacking Police," Boston.com, May 23, 2013.

164. Matt Apuzzo, Michael S. Schmidt, and Julia Preston, "Visa Screening Missed an Attacker's Zealotry on Social Media," *New York Times,* December 13, 2015.

165. Erin Dooley, Becky Perlow, and Jeffrey Cook, "Alleged War Criminal Worked as Security Guard at Dulles Airport, Lawsuit Claims," ABC News, June 2, 2016, available at http://abcnews.go.com/News/alleged -war-criminal-worked-security-guard-dulles-airport/story?id=39535763; Scott Bronstein, Kyra Phillips, and Curt Devine, "He's Accused of War Crimes in Somalia. Now He Works Security at a U.S. Airport," CNN, June 2, 2016, available at http://www.cnn.com/2016/06/01/us/accused-war -criminal-works-at-dulles-airport.

166. Matt Apuzzo, Michael S. Schmidt, and Julia Preston, "Visa Screening Missed an Attacker's Zealotry on Social Media," *New York Times,* December 13, 2015.

167. See, e.g., "Border Patrol Agent Details Immigration Crisis," *Hannity,* Fox News, July 10, 2014, available at http://www.foxnews.com/transcript/2014/ 07/11/border-patrol-agent-details-immigration-crisis; Tim Brown, "Border Agent Ignores Gag Order: Obama Is Aiding, Abetting Illegal Alien Smuggling" (containing CNN video), *Freedom Outpost,* July 4, 2014, available at http://freedomoutpost.com/border-agent-ignores-gag-order-obama-aiding -abetting-fascilitating-illegal-alien-smuggling/#4j7xm6AXoKEJ1veg.99.

168. James Slack, "Conman Blair's Cynical Conspiracy to Deceive the British People and Let in 2 million Migrants Against the Rules:

Explosive New Biography Lays Ex-PM's Betrayal Bare," *The Daily Mail,* February 26, 2016, available at http://www.dailymail.co.uk/news/article-3466485/How-Blair-cynically-let-two-million-migrants-Explosive -biography-reveals-PM-s-conspiracy-silence-immigration-debate.html.

169. Tom Whitehead, "Labour Wanted Mass Immigration to Make UK More Multicultural, Says Former Adviser," *The Telegraph,* October 23 2009, available at http://www.telegraph.co.uk/news/uknews/law -and-order/6418456/Labour-wanted-mass-immigration-to-make-UK-more -multicultural-says-former-adviser.html.

170. James Slack, "Conman Blair's cynical conspiracy to deceive the British people and let in 2 million migrants against the rules: Explosive new biography lays ex-PM's betrayal bare," *Daily Mail,* February 26, 2016.

171. Ibid.

172. Peter Urban, "Dispute over Food Stamps Scuttles Farm Bill in House," *Pawhuska Journal-Capital,* June 26, 2013.

173. Mexican drug cartels are responsible for more than 90 percent of all heroin in the United States. See, e.g., Nick Miroff, "Tracing the U.S. Heroin Surge Back South of the Border As Mexican Cannabis Output Falls," *Washington Post,* April 6, 2014, available at http://www.washing tonpost.com/world/tracing-the-us-heroin-surge-back-south-of-the-border -as-mexican-cannabis-output-falls/2014/04/06/58dfc590-2123-4cc6-b664 -1e5948960576_story.html.

174. Daniel A. Medina, Victor Limjoco, and Kate Snow, "'Our Families Are Dying': New Hampshire's Heroin Crisis," *NBC Nightly News,* February 3, 2016.

175. Fast Facts, National Center for Education Statistics, available at https:// nces.ed.gov/fastfacts/display.asp?id=66.

176. David M. Drucker, "GOP Group Urges 'Tonally, Sensitive' Immigration Messaging," *Congressional Quarterly News,* January 28, 2013.

177. *Fox Special Report with Bret Baier,* Fox News Network, June 16, 2015.

178. Ibid.

179. Ibid.

180. Ibid.

181. See, e.g., Mark Potter, "Border Patrol Faces New Challenge with Surge in Rural Texas Border Crossings," NBC News, May 3, 2013, available at http:// photoblog.nbcnews.com/_news/2013/05/03/17763809-border-patrol-faces -new-challenge-with-surge-in-rural-texas-border-crossings; Steven Camarota, "New Data: Immigration Surged in 2014 and 2015," Center for Immigration Studies, June 2016, available at http://cis.org/New -Data-Immigration-Surged-in-2014-and-2015 ("Mexican immigration has rebounded significantly from the lows of 2010 and 2011"); Caroline May, "Border Surge: Flood of Illegal Immigrants Rising, Exceeding FY 2014 Crisis Levels," Breitbart, May 24, 2016, available at http://www.breitbart.com/big

-government/2016/05/24/border-surge-flood-illegal-immigrants-continue
-rise-exceeding-fy-2014-levels.

182. *Fox Special Report with Bret Baier,* Fox News Network, December 8, 2015.
183. David Brooks, "The American Idea and Today's G.O.P.," *New York Times,* September 25, 2015.
184. John Lantigua, "Before Trump, There Was Nixon and His Divisive Southern Strategy," *Miami Herald,* March 2, 2016.
185. Amanda Taub, "The Rise of American Authoritarianism," *Vox,* March 1, 2016.
186. Sam Quinones, "6 + 4 = 1 Tenuous Existence," *Los Angeles Times,* July 28, 2006, available at http://articles.latimes.com/2006/jul/28/local/me-qua druplets28.
187. "Dramatic Increase of Immigrants in Kentucky," WHAS11, November 28, 2008, available at http://www.topix.com/forum/city/springfield-oh/T0OJL4O560O7B545P; Kelly Foreman, "Criminal Street Gangs Invested in Kentucky," *Kentucky,* Fall 2009, available at https://docjt.ky.gov/Mag azines/Issue%2031/KLE_Feature-On%20the%20Street_Fall%2009.pdf.
188. CNN: Republican Debate, September 16, 2015.
189. *The O'Reilly Factor,* Fox News Network, June 16, 2015.
190. *The O'Reilly Factor,* Fox News Network, August 24, 2015.
191. "Washington Post-ABC News Poll," *Washington Post,* April 10, 2006, available at http://www.washingtonpost.com/wp-srv/politics/polls/postpoll _immigration_041006.htm.
192. Paul Kane, "Boehner Silent on Pathway to Citizenship, Cantor Embraces Tenets of Dream Act," *Post Politics* blog, *Washington Post,* February 5, 2013.
193. Byron Tau and Tarini Parti, "How Big Money Failed Cantor," *Politico,* June 11, 2014, available at http://www.politico.com/story/2014/06/2014 -virginia-primary-big-money-eric-cantor-107699#ixzz48Hew63SF.
194. CNN Live Events/Special: Democratic Debate in Las Vegas, November 17, 2007.
195. CNN: Florida Republican Presidential Debate, January 26, 2012.
196. MSNBC Special: GOP Presidential Debate, September 7, 2011.
197. Ibid.
198. CNN: Republican Debate, September 16, 2015.
199. Ibid.
200. Fox News: Republican Presidential Candidates Debate, August 11, 2011.
201. Ibid.
202. CNN: Republican Debate, September 16, 2015.
203. Fox News: Republican Debate, August 6, 2015.
204. Fox News: Republican Presidential Candidates Debate, August 11, 2011.
205. CNN/Tea Party Express Republican Presidential Debate, September 12, 2011.

206. CNN: GOP Presidential Debate in Las Vegas, December 15, 2015.

207. Fox News: Republican Debate, August 6, 2015.

208. CNN: Republican Debate, September 16, 2015.

209. CNN-Telemundo Republican Presidential Debate, February 26, 2016.

210. MSNBC Special: GOP Presidential Debate, September 7, 2011.

211. CNN: Florida Republican Presidential Debate, January 26, 2012

212. CNN: Republican Debate, September 16, 2015.

213. Fox News: Republican Presidential Candidates Debate, August 11, 2011.

214. MSNBC Special: GOP Presidential Debate, September 7, 2011.

215. CNN: Republican Debate, September 16, 2015.

216. Ian Schwartz, "Trump on Border: Maybe They'll Call It 'The Trump Wall,'" RealClearPolitics, August 19, 2015, available at http://www.real clearpolitics.com/video/2015/08/19/trump_on_border_maybe_theyll_call _it_the_trump_wall.html.

217. "ICE San Antonio Officers Remove Previously Deported Guatemalan Man Who Faces Homicide Charges in Home Country," U.S. Immigration and Customs Enforcement, September 17, 2015, available at https://www.ice .gov/news/releases/ice-san-antonio-officers-remove-previously-deported -guatemalan-man-who-faces-homicide.

218. Thomas B. Edsall, "The Anti-P.C. Vote," New York Times, June 1, 2016, available at http://www.nytimes.com/2016/06/01/opinion/campaign -stops/trump-clinton-edsall-psychology-anti-pc-vote.html.

219. This is what they actually said, verbatim, minus (yet more) irrelevant surplusage:

> JEB!: We need to be much more strategic on how we deal with border enforcement, border security.... There's much to do. And I think rather than talking about this as a wedge issue, which Barack Obama has done now for six long years, the next president, and I hope to be that president, will fix this once and for all so that we can turn this into a driver for high, sustained economic growth.

> KASICH: Donald Trump is hitting a nerve in this country. He is. He's hitting a nerve. People are frustrated. They're fed up. They don't think the government is working for them. And for people who want to just tune him out, they're making a mistake. Now, he's got his solutions. Some of us have other solutions. You know, look, I balanced the federal budget as one of the chief architects when I was in Washington. [*blah, blah, blah*]

> WALLACE: Respectfully, can we talk about illegal immigration?

> KASICH: But the point is that we all have solutions. Mr. Trump is touching a nerve because people want the wall to be built. They want to see an end to illegal immigration. They want to see it, and we all do. But

we all have different ways of getting there. And you're going to hear from all of us tonight about what our ideas are.

RUBIO: Let me set the record straight on a couple of things. The first is, the evidence is now clear that the majority of people coming across the border are not from Mexico. They're coming from Guatemala, El Salvador, Honduras. Those countries are the source of the people that are now coming in its majority. I also believe we need a fence. The problem is if El Chapo builds a tunnel under the fence, we have to be able to deal with that, too. And that's why you need an e-verify system and you need an entry-exit tracking system and all sorts of other things to prevent illegal immigration. But I agree with what Governor Kasich just said. People are frustrated.

BLESSED TRUMP: I would build a great wall—and nobody builds walls better than me, believe me, and I'll build them very inexpensively. I will build a great, great wall on our southern border. And I will have Mexico pay for that wall.

220. Jay Cost, "Republican Party Down," *The Weekly Standard,* May 9, 2016.

221. Ashley Parker and Maggie Haberman, "Donald Trump's Campaign Stumbles as It Tries to Go Big," *New York Times,* May 27, 2016, available at http://www.nytimes.com/2016/05/28/us/politics/donald-trump-campaign.html.

222. Beith Reinhard and Janet Hook, "GOP Operative Plans 'Guerrilla Campaign' Against Donald Trump," *Wall Street Journal,* November 20, 2015, available at http://www.wsj.com/articles/gop-operative-plans-guerrilla-campaign-against-donald-trump-1448050937.

223. Jeremy W. Peters, "G.O.P. Is Weighing Primary Changes After 2016 Chaos," *New York Times,* May 25, 2016.